ALASKA NATIVE CULTURES AND ISSUES

Responses to
Frequently Asked Questions

University of Alaska Press
P.O. Box 756240
Fairbanks, AK 99775-6240

Originally published by the University of Alaska Anchorage and Alaska Pacific

Limit of Liability/Disclaimer of Warranty: While the editors, contributors, and publishers have made their best efforts in preparing this volume, they make no representations or warranties with respect to the accuracy or completeness of the contents. This book is intended as a basic introduction to some very complicated and highly charged questions. Many of the topics are controversial, and all views may not be represented. Interested readers are encouraged to access supplemental readings for a more complete picture.

The first edition was supported in part by a grant from the Alaska Humanities Forum. Any views, findings, conclusions, or recommendations expressed in this publication do not necessarily represent those of the National Endowment for the Humanities.

Library of Congress Cataloging-in-Publication Data

Alaska Native cultures and issues : responses to frequently asked questions / Libby Roderick, editor.
   p. cm.
 Includes bibliographical references and index.
 ISBN 978-1-60223-091-0 (pbk. : acid-free paper)
 1. Indians of North America—Alaska—History. 2. Indians of North America—Alaska—Land tenure. 3. Indians of North America—Alaska—Politics and government. 4. Indians of North America—Alaska—Social conditions. 5. United States. Alaska Native Claims Settlement Act—History. I. Roderick, Libby.
 E78.A3A724 2010
 979.8004'97—dc22
                              2010007912
Cover design by Dixon Jones

This publication was printed on acid-free paper that meets the minimum requirements for ANSI / NISO Z39.48–1992 (R2002) (Permanence of Paper for Printed Library Materials).

ALASKA NATIVE CULTURES AND ISSUES

*Responses to
Frequently Asked Questions*

Edited by Libby Roderick

University of Alaska Press
Fairbanks

INTRODUCTION

This book provides short responses to some frequently asked questions about Alaska Native cultures and issues. It was created because Alaska Native perspectives have too often been misunderstood or ignored, both in higher education and in local, state, and national politics. Again and again, Alaska Native individuals and communities find themselves fielding questions that reveal how little their neighbors understand Alaska Native history, cultures, and concerns. These perspectives are so seldom taught in our schools or addressed in our public life that most of us—Native and non-Native alike—remain unaware of the richness and complexity of the lessons we might learn from them.

The Alaska Native Claims Settlement Act; the cultural centrality of harvesting wild foods (or, as Alaska Native elders refer to it, "our entire way of life"); the legal basis for the Alaska Native health care system; Alaska Native heroes (and villains!); the role of tribal governments and Alaska Native corporations; the historical roots of the social woes that plague many Alaska Native communities; the accomplishments of Alaska Native leaders, artists, and authors; the challenges and opportunities of the future: all of these things and more should be common knowledge for all Alaskans. The lack of such basic understandings can contribute to dire consequences, from ineffective or even disastrous social policies to a sense of disconnection and hopelessness amongst many Alaska Native young people.

This first edition of this volume was created as part of a partnership between the University of Alaska Anchorage and Alaska Pacific University and served as a companion reader for the UAA/APU Books of the Year program in 2008–09. That program in turn grew out of a project sponsored by the Ford Foundation's *Difficult Dialogues* initiative. The two universities have worked together since 2005 to engage faculties and students in more productive ways of discussing controversial topics, ways that both include and respect all perspectives. They have also worked together to begin the long overdue process of more fully honoring and including the expertise, knowledge, and wisdom of Alaska Native cultures and thinkers as part of the university learning experience.

The questions in this book, though hardly exhaustive, are among those most frequently asked and misunderstood by Alaskans. The responses were provided by Alaska-based individuals and scholars within the Anchorage community in addition to and consultation with the UAA/APU Book of the Year committee. Each topic is followed by a list of further readings that may deepen your understanding of these important issues. Online readings (many of them original works, never before published) are available at http://www.uaa.alaska.edu/books-of-the-year/year08-09/supplemental_readings.cfm along with links to materials found on other websites.

Neither the responses nor the readings in this book are intended to speak for all Alaska Native people. Nor do they represent the full range of opinions on any one subject. Nevertheless, the team who created this book has high hopes for it. We hope first that it prompts many Alaskans to investigate the wonderful resources that already exist. We further hope that this collection inspires others to create a truly comprehensive set of resources for teaching and learning about Alaska Native cultures, identities, histories, and issues. Lastly, we hope this volume inspires rich discussions that bring Alaskans a deeper understanding of one another and the issues that affect us all.

Libby Roderick, Editor

ACKNOWLEDGEMENTS

Many people worked very hard to create this book. We deeply appreciate their efforts.

Contributors and Readers

Loren Anderson
Susan Anderson
Bruce Batten
Hallie Bissett
Dr. Jeane Breinig
Dr. Jeanne Eder
Dr. Phyllis Fast
Hazel Felton
Matthew Gilbert
Heather Kendall-Miller
Jim LaBelle
Aaron Leggett
Alexandra J. McClanahan

Dr. Edna Maclean
Helen McNeil
Ilarion (Larry) Merculieff
Paul Ongtooguk
Evon Peter
Libby Roderick
John Shively
Kelly Springer
Vera Starbard
Kristin Tolbert
The Alaska Native Heritage Center
The CIRI Foundation
Southcentral Foundation

Thanks also to: Ray Barnhardt, Brian Brayboy, Debi Bye/Anchorage School District Title VII Indian Education, Doreen Brown, Steve Colt, John Dede, Barbara Hedges, Lisa Jamieson, Randi Madison, Richard Nelson, George Owletuck, Andy Page, Diane Purvis, Lori Seagars, Marie Stewman, Yaso Thiru.

We are especially grateful to Margie Brown for adding her voice to the second edition.

Book of the Year Committee Members

Dr. Jeane Breinig, UAA Department of English
Lauren Bruce, UAA Communication Department
JoAnn Ducharme, UAF Department of Alaska Native and Rural Development
Dr. Phyllis Fast, UAA Anthropology and Liberal Studies
Alexandra McClanahan, Cook Inlet Region, Inc.
Paul Ongtooguk, UAA College of Education
Rosanne Pagano, APU Department of Liberal Studies
Dr. Tim Rawson, APU Department of Liberal Studies
Libby Roderick, Chair, UAA Center for Advancing Faculty Excellence
Dr. Beth Sullivan, APU Rural Alaska Native Adult Distance Education

Editor
Libby Roderick, UAA Center for Advancing Faculty Excellence

Editorial Assistant
Liisa Morrison, UAA Center for Advancing Faculty Excellence

Associate Editor
Kay Landis, UAA Office of the Senior Vice Provost

Copy Editors
Jean Ayers, Independent Clause
Paola Banchero, UAA Department of Journalism and Public Communications

Graphic Design
David Freeman

Photographs
Photos courtesy of Clark James Mishler, Michael Dinneen, David Freeman, the Alaska State Library Historical Collection, and UAA Archive and Special Collections.

Cover
Philip Blanchette and John Chase sing and beat traditional Yup'ik drums at the Alaska Native Heritage Center. Kenny Toovak, Iñupiat Elder from Barrow. Sophia Chya and Serenity Schmidt with traditional Alutiiq headdresses and face tattoos. Photos by Clark James Mishler. Photo of beads by Barry McWayne, University of Alaska Museum of the North.

Map
Language map courtesy of Alaska Native Language Center, University of Alaska Fairbanks.

Special Thanks
To UAA Chancellor Fran Ulmer and APU President Doug North for their support of the UAA/APU Difficult Dialogues partnership and programs, and to Renée Carter-Chapman and Marilyn Barry for their commitment and leadership throughout the project.

TABLE of CONTENTS

Sophia Chya and Serenity Schmidt with traditional Alutiiq headdresses and face tattoos.

Identity, Language, and Culture

Who are Alaska's Native peoples?

What is important to know about Alaska Native cultures?

How many Native languages are there? Is it important to save them?

"First, who we are . . . we are Iñupiaq, Yup'ik, Cup'ik, Siberian Yupik, Tlingit, Haida, Tsimshian, Eyak, Athabascan, Aleut, and Alutiiq. We are the indigenous people of Alaska. For over ten thousand years our ancestors have lived and thrived in one of the harshest areas of the world. We are the last remaining indigenous people in the United States to have never been forcibly removed from our homelands and settled in reservations. We have more than 230 small villages scattered in the largest land mass contained in one state of the union. The residents of many of these Native villages depend on subsistence hunting and fishing to sustain their bodies as well as their traditions and cultures."

Sheri Buretta

Who are Alaska's Native peoples?

The term "Alaska Native" is used to describe the peoples who are indigenous to the lands and waters encompassed by the state of Alaska: peoples whose ancestors have survived here for more than ten thousand years.

Distinct cultural groups. Alaska Native people belong to several major cultural groups— Aleut/Unangan, Athabascan, Eyak, Eskimo (Yup'ik, Cup'ik, Siberian Yupik, Sugpiaq or Alutiiq, Iñupiaq), Haida, Tlingit, Tsimpshian—and many different tribes or clans within those groupings. Each of these cultures is distinct, with complex kinship structures, highly developed subsistence hunting and gathering practices and technologies, and unique and varied languages, belief systems, art, music, storytelling, spirituality, and dance traditions, among many other attributes.

Common values. What these cultural groups share in common, however, are deeply ingrained values, such as honoring the land and waters upon which life depends, having respect and reverence for fish and wildlife, valuing community over individuality, sharing with others, and respecting and learning survival skills and wisdom from elders. Alaska Native cultural worldviews are holistic. Native cultures accept that everything in creation is connected, complex, dynamic, and in a constant state of flux. Alaska Native peoples have a deep and sophisticated qualitative understanding of the environment in which they live. This understanding comes from stories passed down for generations; it also comes from life experiences, learning from mentors beginning at a young age, observations of others in the community, and the guidance of elders.

Geography. The different Alaska Native cultural groups today inhabit the lands they have occupied for more than ten thousand years. The Iñupiaq people live in the Arctic; the Yupiaq live in Southwestern Alaska; the Unungan live in the Aleutian Chain and Pribilof Islands; the Athabascan live in the Interior and Southcentral part of the state; the Tlingit, Haida, and Tsimpshian live in Southeastern Alaska; and the Sugpiaq and Eyak occupy the lower Southcentral region, Kenai Peninsula, and Kodiak. Many now have moved to urban areas, because of economic pressures impinging on the villages and because opportunities for jobs and education are greater in cities. Although it is difficult to estimate the overall Native population in early history, stories and archeological investigations prove that Alaska Native people used and occupied virtually all inhabitable land in the 586,412 square mile terrain we now call Alaska.

Population. Today more than 100,000 Alaska Natives live in Alaska,[1] with many more whose ancestry includes some strand of Alaska Native heritage. Until about 1930, Alaska Native people are estimated to have accounted for between 50 percent and 100 percent of Alaska's population. Due to the influx of non-Natives, however, Alaska Native citizens now represent approximately 16 percent of the state's population.[2] Most live in small rural communities accessible only by air or boat. Roughly 6 percent of Anchorage citizens (approximately 17,000) are of Alaska Native descent.[3] Nearly one-quarter of Alaska schoolchildren from kindergarten through twelfth grade are Alaska Native.[4]

Politics and economics. Alaska Native people are vitally involved in the political and economic landscape of modern Alaska. The Alaska Native Brotherhood (founded in 1912), the Tlingit and Haida Central Council (1939), Alaska Native Sisterhood, the Tundra Times newspaper (1962), the Alaska Federation of Natives (1966), the Inuit Circumpolar Conference (1975), and many other organizations, tribal leaders, Native legislators, and individuals have helped shape key political issues including subsistence, land claims, civil rights, education, cultural and language preservation, energy costs and alternatives, and climate change.

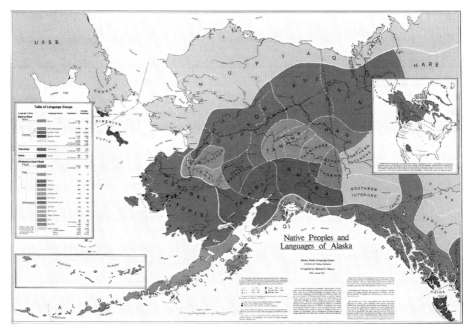

Map courtesy of Alaska Native Language Center, University of Alaska Fairbanks.

3

Following passage of the Alaska Native Claims Settlement Act (ANCSA) in 1971 and establishment of 13 regional and over 200 village corporations, Alaska Native peoples collectively have become among the most powerful economic forces in the state (see pages 19–26). According to the Calista Corporation Report of 2006, Native corporations have combined revenues of more than $4 billion, pouring huge sums into the Alaska economy through job creation, business investments, dividends, and charitable contributions.[5] However, many corporations are still struggling to realize financial gains for shareholders, and many rural Alaska Native people live near poverty levels and depend upon hunting and fishing to survive. Alaska Permanent Fund dividends and government aid are significant sources of income in many rural households.

As history has shown, an understanding of Alaska Native histories and cultures is vital to making wise decisions about Alaska's environment, public education, and economy. Readings in this section help explain some aspects of Alaska Native identities and cultures and the role they play in shaping Alaska today and tomorrow.

What is important to know about Alaska Native cultures?

An attempt to answer this question fully has engaged many scholars, elders, and educators for hundreds of years. Here are some fundamentals:

Alaska Native cultures:
- have developed over thousands of years in response to environmental conditions among the most challenging on earth.
- are many and varied, representing at least seven major groups across the state—Aleut/ Unangan (Southwestern Coastal Alaska), Iñupiaq (Northwestern and Northern Coastal), Athabascan (Interior), Tlingit (Southeastern), Tsimpshian (Southeastern), Haida (Southeastern), Eyak (Southeastern), Yup'ik, Cup'ik, Siberian Yupik, Sugpiaq/Alutiiq (Southwestern), with many different tribes or clans within those groupings.
- are distinct from one another, with unique and varied languages; complex kinship structures; and highly developed art, music, storytelling, belief systems, spiritual practices, educational systems, dance traditions, and subsistence hunting and gathering practices and technologies.
- share key values, such as honoring the land and waters upon which life depends; respecting and sharing with others; respecting and learning from elders; living with an attitude of humility and patience; honoring the interconnections among all things; being

mindful in word and deed; and knowing one's place within one's history, traditions, and ancestors.

- are completely rooted in and tied to the land and waters of a particular region and the practices and customs necessary to thrive in that region.
- have been hard hit by myriad forces over the past two centuries, including diseases brought by European immigrants and traders; enslavement and/or oppression by colonizing powers (including the United States government, territorial government, Russian government, and religious organizations); a huge influx of non-Natives, which has altered access to subsistence foods and resulted in restrictive regulation; the arrival of western technologies, religions, economic systems, industrial development, and educational systems; and climate change.

Despite these obstacles, Alaska's Native peoples not only continue to survive, but also help define Alaska's economy, politics, and future.

It is important to note that traveling to the remote villages where most Alaska Native people live is, for non-Natives, like traveling to a foreign country in every sense of the word. A casual observer may note that Alaska Native individuals appear to be "Americanized" in that they use modern tools, clothes, machinery, and speak English. But the bulk of Alaska Native identity is beneath the surface. Each village has different relationship and communication protocols, different customs and traditions, and different worldviews even within a single region of Alaska; these differences are magnified when considered against other indigenous cultures and mainstream society.

"For far too long we Dena'ina people have been trying to tell our story in other people's words. This may explain some of why we've been almost invisible in our own country, even among ourselves."

Clare Swan

Alaska Native peoples have had intimate contact with their immediate environments for hundreds of generations and thus have a profound understanding of place. Development of oil reserves on Alaska's North Slope in the 1970s introduced a new tension when Alaska Native aboriginal land claims impeded construction of the 800-mile Trans-Alaska Pipeline. Most Alaska Native land claims were extinguished by congressional action in 1971, a solution that remains a topic of dispute today (see section on ANCSA, pages 19–26).

Alaska Native history is fraught with stories of conflict with western legal systems (particularly over land) and with western theories about land, fish, and wildlife, as well as individual versus communal rights—struggles some Native people believe may only heighten as Alaska continues to attract newcomers who know little, if anything, about Alaska's first peoples.

Alaska's Native peoples have a deep understanding and wisdom about fish, wildlife, habitat, weather, climate, and geography that could benefit all peoples. As environmental issues grow ever more daunting—even threatening the survival of all life on this planet— Alaska Native cultures, worldviews, knowledge, and wisdom offer alternatives for living in a respectful and sustainable relationship with the natural world.

How many Native languages are there?
Is it important to save them?

Alaska is home to twenty Alaska Native languages, along with a multitude of regional dialects. In Native cultures, as in every culture, language serves as a vessel for entire ways of thinking and relating to the world. It is a storehouse of accumulated knowledge, wisdom, information, beliefs, history, and identity; it reveals its speakers' philosophical views, sense of place, social relationships, political organization, learning styles, and attitudes about everything from food to land to marriage to spirituality. Language expresses the unique cumulative experience of a group of people over generations and offers the rest of the human race another view of how to live in the world.

From the perspective of indigenous people, language is birthed from the land in which the people themselves live and contains the vibration of these lands in the sounds of the words used. Each spoken tongue is unique: the result of thousands of years of living in a specific area. An adopted or second language can never replicate what a particular indigenous language can communicate.

Alaska Native words and languages are multidimensional in meaning. Some words or phrases communicate not only information, but also spiritual and emotional dimensions reflective of the holistic worldview of Alaska Native peoples. This is why Alaska Native elders often speak in their own language rather than in English in group settings, even when speaking to an English-only group. To them, the English language cannot convey the depth of meaning their own language can.

The destruction or erosion of the languages of Native peoples all around the planet is of central concern to indigenous nations, anthropologists, linguists, and people of all backgrounds who understand the value and necessity of preserving cultural, linguistic, and intellectual diversity on behalf of the human future. Of the 6,000 languages spoken around the globe, linguists fear that up to 90 percent could disappear by the next century.

Native languages in Alaska are suffering some of the greatest losses. Out of the twenty languages, seventeen have 300 or fewer speakers remaining.[6] Marie Smith Jones, chief of the Eyak nation and the last surviving speaker of the Eyak language (a 3,000-year-old language from Southcentral Alaska), died in January 2008. Although she and others worked very hard to pass the Eyak language on to the next generation, there is now no one alive today for whom Eyak was a primary tongue and fundamental way of understanding the world.

Native languages have been endangered or eroded by the forces of colonization for the past several hundred years. Beginning with their arrival in the 1700s, many missionaries, government officials, and educators actively promoted policies and practices aimed at destroying or marginalizing the languages spoken by Native peoples, acting on the misguided belief that forcing Alaska Native peoples to abandon their traditional ways and become like "white" people was a progressive act. With a few notable exceptions, most mission or boarding schools (including those once attended by many living Native adults), forbade Native children from speaking their own languages and harshly punished them if they persisted. By breaking the linguistic bonds that tied children to their cultures and elders, a chasm opened up between many Alaska Native elders and youth. Much vital knowledge and wisdom was lost.

Unlike immigrants to the United States who gave up their original languages to assimilate, indigenous peoples of the United States have no country of origin to which they may return and in which their native tongue is still being spoken. Italian-Americans may return to an Italy in which their traditional language is still actively used; Chinese dialects are still alive to Chinese-Americans who wish to reconnect with linguistic and cultural roots. Without denying the losses and struggles that descendants of immigrant groups face, it must be acknowledged that Alaska Native peoples are in a very different position.

> "Human relationships are embedded in the grammar and become a subconscious part of the … soul … If we are to truly understand this place, we have to understand the language of this place."
>
> Alan Boraas

Alaska Native peoples are living on their ancestral lands; if they lose their cultures, lands, or languages, there is nowhere else to return to. Those languages, and the ways of living, connecting to, and viewing the world they represent, will be lost forever.

In spite of efforts to marginalize Alaska Native languages (such as the "English-only" laws passed overwhelmingly by voters in 1998, which sought to require that all official businesses in the villages take place in English alone), many efforts have been underway for the past few decades to document and pass on Alaska Native languages. Many schools throughout Alaska now offer bilingual programs. The Fairbanks-based Alaska Native Language Center and a host of other sites offer online resources. A few university-level language classes are offered throughout the state.

Many oral history projects seek to document the speech of elders from various regions, and Alaska Native elders and leaders throughout the state are encouraging young people to learn to speak their original languages. Being able to speak both English and traditional languages is a strength that will allow these young people to walk in two worlds and retain a valuable heritage for their children and the rest of humanity.

1. Alaska Department of Labor & Workforce Development. 2006. "Alaska Population Projections 2007-2030." http://www.labor.state.ak.us/ research/pop/projections/AKNativePopProj.xls#AlaskaNative!A1

2. Statewide Library Electronic Doorway. http://sled.alaska.edu/akfaq/aknatpop.html

3. U.S. Census Bureau. 2006. Quick Facts. http://quickfacts.census.gov/qfd/states/02/02020.html

4. Department of Education Alaska Department of Education and Early Development. "Accountability and Assessment Total Statewide Enrollment by Ethnicity, Grade and Percent as of October 1, 2006." www.eed.state.ak.us/stats/StatewidebyEthnicity/2007Statewide_Gr_X_Ethnicity.pdf

5. McClanahan, Alexandra J. "Alaska Native Corporations — Ch'etbuja: We Share It, A Look at 13 Native Regional Corporations and 13 Native Village Corporations." 2006. Association of ANCSA Regional Corporation Presidents/CEOs. http://www.calistacorp.com/docs/reports/ANCSA_CEO_Report2006.pdf

6. Krauss, Michael. "The Vanishing Languages of the Pacific Rim," *Anchorage Daily News*, Wed. Jan 23, 2008, page A10.

"Languages . . . shape thought and epistemological modes of learning. Take this Iñupiaq term: *aavzuuk*. First, it is a complete sentence meaning 'constellation consisting of two stars which appear above the horizon in late December, an indication that the solstice is past and that days will soon grow longer again.' . . . Structurally polysynthetic, the Iñupiaq language allows the speaker to economize on sound to maximize meaning with simply inclusion and replacement of key morphemes. Such morphemes are explicit in terms of direction, number of speakers, number of listeners, height from the horizon line, and time. Second, in this example Iñupiaq epistemology makes use of language to impart astronomical knowledge of the constellations, calendric data, and patience about the presence or absence of light. Implied within the term, *aavzuuk*, is the suggestion that the Iñupiaq speaker will learn what to expect of the environment and other creatures in it at this time of year. Thus, the Iñupiaq sense of a maturing self grows with knowledge of the language."

Dr. Phyllis Fast

Blanket toss at the World Eskimo Olympics in Fairbanks.

READINGS

Please visit our web site at
**http://www.uaa.alaska.edu/books-of-the-year/
year08-09/supplemental_readings.cfm**
for a variety of supplemental readings

Online Readings

Bissett, Hallie. "I am Alaska Native."
UAA graduate and MBA student Dena'ina Athabascan Hallie Bissett discusses her struggle of coming to terms with and realizing the importance of her indigenous identity.

Breinig, Jeane. "Alaska Native Writers, Alaska Native Identities."
Jeane Breinig, Ph.D., Haida, is currently a UAA Associate Professor of English. In this essay,
Breinig discusses how four Alaska Natives writers portray aspects of their contemporary identities,
while still maintaining connections to their respective cultural traditions.

Breinig, Jeane. "Inside the Circle of a Story." LitSite Alaska. http://www.litsite.org
This family story discusses the role of Haida oral traditions, storytelling, and language revitalization
in Southeast Alaska. It includes links to writing by Dr. Breinig's mother, Julie Coburn.

Bruchac, Joseph W. III. "We Are the In-betweens: An Interview with Mary TallMountain." In *Studies
in American Indian Literatures* 1, no. 1 (Summer 1989).
Interview with renowned Koyukon-Athabascan writer, adopted into a white family at the age of six.

Burch, Ernest S., Jr. "From Skeptic to Believer: The Making of an Oral Historian." In *Alaska History*
6, no. 1 (Spring 1991).
Ernie Burch, Jr., Ph.D., social anthropologist, specializes in the early historic social organization
of the Iñupiaq. In this essay, he argues for the validity of using Native oral histories to truly understand the historical record. He contends that oral histories are often ignored or misunderstood by
academics, and argues for their inclusion in research projects.

Davis, Robert. "Saginaw Bay: I Keep Going Back." In *Alaska Quarterly Review* 26, nos. 1–2 (Spring/
Summer 2009).

Fast, Phyllis. "Alaska Native Language, Culture, and Identity." 2008.
Phyllis Fast, Ph.D., Athabascan, is a UAA Associate Professor of Anthropology, author, and art-
ist. In this essay, Fast discusses the value of pre-colonial religious traditions and language, as well
as the post-colonial impact of the Alaska Native Claims Settlement Act (ANCSA) of 1971 and the
ANCSA 1991 Amendments of 1988.

Garza, Dolly. "The Origins of 'Tlingit Moon and Tide.'" LitSite Alaska. http://www.litsite.org
Dolly Garza, Ph.D., Tlingit and Haida, explains educational and cultural functions of a Tlingit story.

Hensley, Willie. Speech at Bilingual Conference, Anchorage, February 1981.
William Hensley, Iñupiaq, architect of ANCSA, reflects on key issues regarding the relationship between schooling, education, and the future of Alaska Native cultures in a 1981 speech to the annual Bilingual/ MultiEducation Conference.

Jacobson, Steven A. "Central Yup'ik and the Schools." Alaska Native Language Center, Juneau: 1984.
This handbook was designed to assist school districts in providing effective educational services to students from the Yup'ik language group. This is one of three handbooks developed to increase school districts' and school personnel's understanding of certain Alaska Native language groups.

Maclean, Edna Ahgeak. "Why Don't We Give Our Children to Our Native Languages?"
Edna Maclean, Ph.D., Iñupiaq, former president of Iligsavik College, provides an overview of the effects of education on Alaska Native languages, a discussion of the State of Alaska's approach to bilingual education, and suggestions for ways to revive and maintain Alaska Native languages.

Oquilluk, William. *People of Kauwerak: Legends of the Northern Eskimo.* Alaska Pacific University, 1981.
William Oquilluk, Iñupiaq from Point Hope (1896–1972), wrote down these stories of his people when he was concerned they would be lost without written documentation. This excerpt from his book focuses on one of the disasters that befell his people.

TallMountain, Mary. "Indian Blood." *The Language of Life: A Festival of Poets.* Bill Moyers, ed. Anchor, 1996.
Poem by nationally renowned Koyukon-Athabascan writer.

Thompson, Chad. *Athabaskan Languages and the Schools: A Handbook for Teachers.* Jane McGary, ed. Alaska Native Language Center, 1984.
Chad Thompson, Ph.D., linguist, describes the job of a linguist and provides an overview of Athabascan languages.

Williams, Brad. "A Bridge Between Two Worlds: The Term Half Breed Gets a New Definition." In *True North* (Spring 1999):10-14.
Brad Williams, reporter for *True North*, interviews several "mixed identity" Alaska Native citizens, including Jack Dalton, Tim Gilbert, and Priscilla Hensley.

Other Web Sites of Interest

Alaska Native Language Center. http://www.uaf.edu/anlc/
Internationally recognized, the ANLC was established in 1972 by state legislation as a center for documentation and cultivation of the state's twenty Native languages. Housed at the University

of Alaska Fairbanks, ANLC publishes research in story collections, dictionaries, grammars, and research papers. ANLC also maintains an archival collection of more than 10,000 items.

Sealaska Heritage Institute.
Online resources promoting language restoration of Tlingit, Haida, and Tsimpshian languages.
http://www.tlingitlanguage.org/
http://www.haidalanguage.org/
http://www.tsimshianlanguage.org/

Hard Copy Readings

Breinig, Jeane. "Alaskan Haida Narratives: Maintaining Cultural Identity Through Subsistence." *Telling the Stories: Essays on American Indian Literatures and Cultures.* Malcolm A. Nelson and Elizabeth Hoffman Nelson, eds. Peter Lang Publishing, 2001.

Breinig, Jeane. "Alaskan Haida Stories of Language Growth and Regeneration." In *American Indian Quarterly* 30 (Winter/Spring 2006):110–118.

Brown, Emily Ivanoff. *The Roots of Ticasuk: An Eskimo Woman's Family Story.* Portland: Alaska Northwest Publishing Company, 1981.
> Collection of stories by Ivanoff. Revision of master's thesis from University of Alaska. Orginally published as *Grandfather of Unalakleet* (1974).

Brown, Emily Ivanoff. *Tales of Ticasuk: Eskimo Legends and Stories.* Fairbanks: University of Alaska Press, 1987.
> Emily Ivanoff Brown (1904–1982), of Unalakleet, was a grade-school teacher and advocate of bilingual education. She is recognized by Alaska Native people as an important educator. Emily's Native name ("Ticasuk") means, "Where the four winds gather their treasures from all parts of the world…the greatest of which is knowledge." This book is a collection of her writings, focusing on the oral stories of her people.

Bruchac, Joseph, ed. *Raven Tells Stories.* Greenfield Center: Greenfield Review Press, 1991.
> Collection of creative writing (primarily poetry) which includes briefs interviews with selected authors who address aspects of their contemporary Native identity. Also includes biographies and writings by Tlingit writers Robert Davis and Diane Benson, among others.

Christianson, Susan Stark. *Historical Profile of the Central Council: Tlingit and Haida Indian Tribes of Alaska.* Revised edition. Central Council Tlingit and Haida Indian Tribes of Alaska, 1992.
> Early history of the movement of the Tlingit and Haida peoples to keep their traditional lifestyle and ancestral lands.

Crowell, Aron L., Amy P. Steffian, and Gordon L. Pullar, eds. *Looking Both Ways: Heritage and Identity of the Alutiiq People*. Fairbanks: University of Alaska Press, 2001.
> Combines the archaeology, history, and oral tradition of the Alutiiq people to trace a path through ancestral generations to contemporary life.

Dauenhauer, Nora M. *Life Woven with Song*. Tucson: University of Arizona Press, 2000.
> Collection of poems, plays and essays by noted Tlingit scholar. Provides readers with creative expressions of Dauenhauer's cultural traditions.

Dauenhauer, Nora, and Richard Dauenhauer, eds. *Haa Kusteeyí, Our Culture: Tlingit Life Stories: Classics of Tlingit Oral Literature* 3. Seattle: University of Washington Press, 1994.
Recommended excerpts:
> ■ "Introduction: The Context of Tlingit Biography" (pp. 3–23), including "Tlingit Geography and Social Structure" and "The Concept of At.óow" (Tlingit culture and its understanding of ownership and belonging).
> ■ Pages 525–544.

Dauenhauer, Nora, and Richard Dauenhauer, eds. *Haa Shuká, Our Ancestors: Tlingit Oral Narratives*. Seattle: University of Washington Press and Sealaska Heritage, 1987.
Recommended excerpt:
> ■ Story told by Susie James about Glacier Bay history.

Dunham, Mike. "Voice for the Voiceless: Mary TallMountain." In *Anchorage Daily News,* Lifestyles, November 13, 1994.
> Story about nationally renowned Koyukon-Athabascan writer (1918–1994), adopted at age six due to the tuberculosis that ravaged Alaska and her village. The story describes the obstacles she overcame, her return to Alaska, and how she used writing as a form of healing. Examples of her creative writing are included: "Indian Blood" and "You Can Go Home Again."

Fast, Phyllis Ann. "Footprints: Metaphors of Place, Mobility, and History." *Northern Athabascan Survival: Women, Community, and the Future*. Lincoln: University of Nebraska Press, 2002.
> This chapter discusses Northern Athabascan history in terms of its impact on Athabascan women, the economy, and leadership in the aftermath of colonial encounters.

Fienup-Riordan, Ann, William Tyson, Paul John, Marie Meade, and John Active. "Metaphors of Conversion/Metaphors of Change." *Hunting Tradition in a Changing World: Yup'ik Lives in Alaska Today*. New Brunswick: Rutgers University Press, 2000.
> Ann Fienup-Riordan, Ph.D., is a cultural anthropologist and independent scholar celebrated for her work with the Yup'ik. This chapter examines what different people in Yup'ik villages have said about change in their communities, with close attention paid to their use of metaphor.

Fienup-Riordan, Ann. *The Nelson Island Eskimo Social Structure and Ritual Distribution*. Anchorage: Alaska Pacific University Press, 1983.

Recommended excerpt:

"Ethnographic Setting" (pp. 1–28) gives an overview of Qaluyaaq—Nelson Island—including its geography and an overview of the historical period up to the 1930s.

Fienup-Riordan, Ann, and Lawrence D. Kaplan, eds. *Words of the Real People: Alaska Native Literature in Translation.* Fairbanks: University of Alaska Press, 2007.

Collection of life stories, poetry, and oral literature of the Yup'ik, Iñupiaq, and Alutiiq peoples accompanied by background essays on each Native group.

Fienup-Riordan, Ann. "The Real People and the Children of Thunder" and "Yup'ik Warfare and the Myth of the Peaceful Eskimo." *Eskimo Essays: Yup'ik Lives and How We See Them.* New Brunswick: Rutgers University Press, 1990.

These two chapters focus on the effects of Western contact and traditional Yup'ik worldviews.

Hayes, Ernestine. *Blonde Indian: An Alaska Native Memoir.* Tucson: University of Arizona Press, 2006.

Ernestine Hayes, Assistant Professor of English at UAA Southeast, won the American Book Award for this memoir. *Blonde Indian* combines Tlingit storytelling with the author's personal life story.

Hensley, William L. Iggiagruk. *Fifty Miles from Tomorrow: A Memoir of Alaska and the Real People.* New York: Farrar, Straus and Giroux, 2008.

Memoir of Willie Hensley, Iñupiaq leader who grew up on the shores of Kotzebue Sound.

John, Peter. *The Gospel According to Peter John.* Fairbanks: Alaska Native Knowledge Network, University of Alaska Fairbanks, 1996.

Peter John (1900–2003) was elected in 1992 by Athabascan elders to be their traditional chief. He testified in favor of Native land claims in the late 1960s and advocated sobriety for Alaska Native peoples. This book is an edited compilation of oral interviews with David Krupa, undertaken as a way to share his spiritual insight of combining his traditional values with Christianity.

Kari, James, and Alan Boraas, eds. *A Dena'ina Legacy—K'tl'egh'i Sukdu: The Collected Writings of Peter Kalifornsky.* Fairbanks: Alaska Native Language Center, University of Alaska Fairbanks, 1991.

Collection of 147 bilingual Dena'ina-English writings by self-taught writer and scholar Peter Kalifornsky of Kenai (1911–1993), who focused on bringing back Dena'ina as a living language in Southcentral Alaska.

Recommended excerpt: "Peter Kalifornsky: A Biography by Alan S. Boraas" (pp. 470–481) gives a short biography of Kalifornsky and a brief history of the region.

Kari, James. *Shem Pete's Alaska: The Territory of the Upper Cook Inlet Dena'ina.* Fairbanks: University of Alaska Press, 2003.

James Kari, Ph.D., retired linguist, worked with Shem Peter and more than forty other Dena'ina and Ahtna Athabascan people on this landmark book connecting the language, landscape, and Dena'ina people of the upper Cook Inlet. One of the finest examples of the way oral history can be used to connect the naming of places and the stories associated with geographic features to a people's history.

Mather, Elsie. "With a Vision Beyond Our Immediate Needs." *When Our Words Return: Writing, Hearing and Remembering Oral Traditions of Alaska and the Yukon*. P. Morrow and W. Schneider, eds. Logan: Utah University Press, 1995. 20–26.
>   Elsie Mather, Yup'ik educator, describes the ways English grammatical and pedagogical models have often overlooked and undermined Alaska Native oral traditions. In this essay, she tries to come to grips with the "necessary monster" of literacy in relation to her Yup'ik language and cultural ideals.

McClanahan, Alexandra J. *Our Stories, Our Lives*. Anchorage: CIRI Foundation, 1986.
>   Collection of personal experiences and traditional stories told by twenty-three Alaska Native elders of the Cook Inlet Region in Southcentral Alaska who witnessed dramatic cultural changes in Alaska 1900–1985. Compiled and edited by noted CIRI historian Alexandra J. McClanahan.

McClanahan, Alexandra J., Aaron Leggett, and Lydia L. Hays. *Dena'ina: Nat'uh/Our Special Place*. Anchorage: Cook Inlet Tribal Council, Inc., 2007.
>   Story about the indigenous people of Cook Inlet region includes the early Kachemak Tradition people, focusing on the Dena'ina Athabascan people.
>   Recommended excerpts:
>   ■ "Na Tikahtnu Sukdu: Our Cook Inlet Story" (p. 9), by Clare Swan, describes the need for Native people to tell history in their own words.
>   ■ "Dena'ina: Nat'uh, Our Special Place" (pp. 15–19) provides overview of Cook Inlet/Tikahtnu indigenous history.

Natives of Alaska. *Alaska Native Ways: What the Elders Have Taught Us*. Portland: Graphic Arts Center Publishing Company, 2002.
>   Alaska Native individuals discuss how they carry their traditional values into the contemporary world. With an introduction by Will Mayo and color photographs by Roy Corral.

Nolan, Maia. "Premiere of One-Man Show About Race Compelling, Honest." In *Anchorage Daily News*, November 8, 2007.
>   Review of *My Heart Runs in Two Directions at Once*, one-man performance by storyteller Jack Dalton, half Yup'ik and half European-American, and his efforts to find and honor his full identity.

Oleksa, Michael. "Elizabeth Peratrovich and Roy Peratrovich." *Haa Kusteeyí, Our Culture: Tlingit Life Stories: Classics of Tlingit Oral Literature* 3. Nora Marks Dauenhauer and Richard Dauenhauer, eds. Seattle: University of Washington Press, 1994. 525–544.
>   Brief biography of Roy and Elizabeth Peratrovich and an overview of their fight for equal rights.

Orth, Donald J. *Dictionary of Alaska Place Names*. US Geological Survey, 1971.
>   Detailed compendium of geographic names for places and features of the Alaska landscape.
>   Recommended excerpt:
>   ■ "Sources of Names" (pp. 6–44) provides overview of military expeditions, explorers, and government studies that led to the mapping of Alaska.

Price, Robert E. *The Great Father in Alaska: The Case of the Tlingit and Haida Salmon Fishery.* Douglas: First Street Press, 1990.

A study of federal Indian policy and political history of the indigenous people of Southeast Alaska since 1867, wth a focus on the salmon industry.

Raboff, Adeline Peter. *Iñuksuk: Northern Koyukon, Gwich'in & Lower Tanana 1800–1901.* Alaska Native Knowledge Network, 2001.

History of the Northern Koyukon, Western Gwich'in and Lower Tanana kept by storytellers for over one hundred and fifty years. Accounts taken from written records of the early explorers, traders, missionaries, and the oral tradition of the Alaska Native peoples themselves. Available through the University of Alaska Press.

Recommended excerpts:

■ "The Archeological Record" (pp. 33–38) discusses the long-held belief that the central Brooks Range area was solely Iñupiat between 1250 and 1850, while evidence suggests that the area supported a significant Athasbascan population during that time.

■ "Northern Koyukon, Gwich'in, and Lower Tanana Timeline" (pp. 169–171) provides timeline of the region, 1250–1898.

Spatz, Ronald, Jeane Breinig, and Patricia Partnow, eds. *Alaska Native Writers, Storytellers and Orators: The Expanded Edition. Alaska Quarterly Review* 25, nos 3–4. University of Alaska Anchorage, 1999.

Anthology of Alaska Native oral and written texts, including both traditional stories in the respective languages with facing translations and contemporary creative texts written in English. It also features a "Contexts" section which provides cultural, historical, and literary background for the selections.

Stephan, A.E. *The First Athabascans of Alaska: Strawberries.* Pittsburgh: Dorrance Publishing Co., 1996.

In an effort to retain the valuable history of her ancestors, tribal Elder A.E. Stephan documents the story of the Athabascans.

Recommended excerpts:

"The First Athabascans of Alaska: Strawberries" (pp. 5–6). Overview of Cook Inlet history.

"Indian Society" (pp. 9–12). Dena'ina culture, potlatches.

"Indian Beliefs" (pp. 15–16). Overview of spirituality.

TallMountain, Mary. *The Light on the Tent Wall: A Bridging.* Los Angeles: University of California American Indian Studies Center, 1990.

Collection of poetry and prose by nationally recognized Koyukon-Athabascan writer.

TallMountain, Mary. "You Can Go Home Again." *I Tell You Now: Autobiographical Essays by Native American Writers.* Brian Swann and Arnold Krupat, eds. University of Nebraska Press, 1987.

Essay by nationally renowned Koyukon-Athabascan writer, adopted out of her family at six due to the tuberculosis that ravaged Alaska and her village.

Wallis, Velma. *Bird Girl and the Man Who Followed the Sun*. Kenmore: Epicenter Press, 2003.
Renowned author of national bestseller *Two Old Women*, Velma Wallis, Gwich'in Athabascan, interweaves two classic Athabascan oral tales. This is the story of two rebels who break the strict taboos of their communal culture in their quest for freedom and adventure. The text raises interesting questions about gender and identity.

Wallis, Velma. *Raising Ourselves*, Kenmore: Epicenter Press, 2003.
A coming of age tale. Gritty, but inspiring.

Other Resources

MacLean, Andrew Okpeaha. "Sikumi" (On the Ice).
A short feature film of a hunter who goes out on the ice looking for seal and inadvertently witnesses a murder. Winner of 2008 Jury Prize in Short Filmmaking at the Sundance Film Festival, 2008.

Span, Laura Bliss. "More than Words: The Life and Language of Eyak Chief Marie Smith." 60 minute video. http://findarticles.com/p/articles/mi_m0GER/is_2000_Spring/ai_61426211

Cook Inlet Region Incorporated (CIRI) headquarters, Anchorage, Alaska.

Alaska Native Claims Settlement Act and Corporations

What is the Alaska Native Claims Settlement Act (ANCSA)?

How did Alaska Native corporations start up?

Do all Alaska Native people get dividends?

What do Alaska Native people think of ANCSA?

"We are not asking for anything. We are offering the U.S. Government 84 percent of our property. We are offering them...more than 300 million acres to satisfy the needs of others in the state and to satisfy the needs of the United States in the way of federal reserves, wildlife refuges, wilderness areas. We will accommodate them all. We are asking merely to be able to retain 16 percent of our land in each region and we are asking for extinguishment of title to the other 300 million acres, $500 million from the Congress and 2 percent royalty in perpetuity which will be utilized over the whole state of Alaska."

Don Wright

What is the Alaska Native Claims Settlement Act (ANCSA)?

The Alaska Native Claims Settlement Act (ANSCA) is an historic piece of legislation enacted in 1971 to resolve disputes between Alaska Native people and the U.S. government over ownership and development of traditional Native lands. One of the most significant outcomes of this legislation was the creation of Alaska Native corporations (see following question, page 22).

Alaska Native peoples have been living for thousands of years on the lands now called Alaska (a westernized version of the Aleut term for "great land" or "mainland"). Current theory asserts that early peoples migrated to Alaska some 25,000 years ago over a land bridge connecting Alaska and eastern Siberia.[1] These immigrants then spread out over the region, developing over time into multiple, distinct nations.

In the 1700s, traders from other nations—Russia, Spain, England, and what would become the United States—arrived in increasing numbers to exploit the fur trade. In 1784, Russia asserted dominion and claimed Alaska as a colony.

In 1867, Russia sold Alaska to the United States government for $7,200,000 (about 1.9¢ per acre), transferring title to all "public and vacant" lands not owned by individuals, without regard to the claims of aboriginal peoples who had been living on the lands for generations. These peoples—deemed "uncivilized tribes" by the United States government—considered most of these lands to be their communal property, based on the principle of "traditional use and occupancy." The treaty with Russia "provided that those tribes would be subject to such laws and regulations as the United States might from time to time adopt with respect to aboriginal tribes."[2]

In 1884, Congress declared that indigenous Americans "should not be disturbed in the possession of any lands actually in their use or occupation or then claimed by them, but that the terms under which such persons could acquire title to such lands were reserved for future legislation by Congress."[3] This action was significant because it laid a groundwork for Native land claims that, in Alaska, would take another century to resolve.

In 1966, Alaska Native leaders convened statewide as the Alaska Federation of Natives (AFN), an entity that meets annually and remains a political force today. AFN pressed Congress to resolve the question of Alaska Native land claims stemming in part from Alaska's days as a Russian colony and United States territory. From the perspective of many Native individuals and organizations, the lands on which they had been living and subsisting from "time immemorial" had never been the property of Russia to sell. Pressure was building to settle aboriginal claims: the state wanted resolution to carry out day-to-day affairs, and construction of the $8 billion Trans-Alaska Pipeline could not go ahead until conflicting land claims were settled.

After five years of struggle and compromise among Alaska Native groups, the state, oil companies, and conservationists, the ANSCA was passed by Congress and signed into law by President Richard Nixon.

Until ANCSA, official U.S. policy had been to "grant to them [indigenous people] title to a portion of the lands which they occupied, to extinguish the aboriginal title to the remainder of the lands by placing such lands in the public domain, and to pay the fair value of the titles extinguished."[4] (This policy was frequently dishonored, however; a cursory review of Native American history indicates numerous incidences of indigenous groups being forcibly removed from their homelands without remuneration.)

In the fall of 1970, then Secretary of the Interior Walter Hickel met with prominent figures in the Alaska Land Claims dispute in his Washington office. Clockwise from far left: Wally Hickel; Tim Wallis, President Fairbanks Native Association; Charles (Etok) Edwardson, Executive Director Arctic Slope Native Association; Eben Hopson, Barrow; Emil Notti; Attorney Barry Jackson (standing); State Senator William Hensley; Alfred Ketzler, Nenana; Barbara Trigg, Nome; unknown; Delois Ketzler; Harvey Samuelson, Dillingham; George Miller, Kenai; unknown; State Senator Ray C. Christiansen (far right); Frank Degnan, Unalakleet; Moses Paukan; Morris Thompson; John Borbridge (back to camera).

How did Alaska Native corporations start up?

Passage of ANCSA on December 18, 1971, provided title to forty million acres to be divided among some 220 Native villages and twelve regions within the state. An additional four million acres consisting of historical sites, gravesites, and other special lands were made available with certain constraints on usage: economic development was to be restricted on these lands. Twelve regional and over 200 village corporations—entirely new structures in Native societies—were set up to select the lands, hold the titles, and receive, invest, and administer the settlement payments on behalf of their shareholders. A thirteenth corporation was set up to receive monies on behalf of Alaska Native people living outside the state. These corporations shared in a payment of $462 million over an eleven-year period, and an additional $500 million in oil revenues derived from specified Alaska lands.[5]

ANCSA Regional Corporations

Ahtna, Incorporated

The Aleut Corporation (TAC)

Arctic Slope Regional Corporation (ASRC)

Bering Straits Native Corporation (BSNC)

Bristol Bay Native Corporation (BBNC)

Calista Corporation

Chugach Alaska Corporation (CAC)

Cook Inlet Region, Inc. (CIRI)

Doyon Limited

Koniag, Incorporated

NANA Regional Corporation (NANA)

Sealaska Corporation

The 13th Regional Corporation

Alaska Native people who were born on or before December 18, 1971 and enrolled in the corporations became shareholders—another new concept and relationship for most of them. Under ANCSA, most village corporations retained only surface rights to the lands they selected, with regional corporations responsible for managing subsurface resources found on their lands and the lands of the village corporations within their regions. If those subsurface resources were developed (i.e. mined, drilled), 70 percent of the revenues generated were to be shared among all twelve regional corporations and all of the village corporations on a per capita basis—a very different arrangement compared with non-Native corporations across the globe.

From the outset, as holders of the last remaining Alaska Native lands, the village and regional corporations have assumed enormous responsibilities. They have also faced enormous challenges, including an initial shortage of well-prepared Alaska Native people ready to operate these new and complex structures. Like all other corporations, Native corporations strive to maximize profits for their shareholders and may be liable for mismanagement if they fail to do so. Many regional corporations have invested in real estate, secured military contracts, and engaged in mining, logging and other economic endeavors to generate corporate profits. A few corporations earn large profits from their efforts; many are only modestly profitable. Others have so far failed to attain profitability but nevertheless continue to survive.

This arrangement introduces a unique tension between profitable and unprofitable corporations. Even more potentially divisive is the question of who gets to own shares in the corporations at all, especially when it comes to Alaska Native people born after 1971.

Do all Alaska Native people get dividends?

The short answer is no. ANCSA corporations declare dividends only in years when they make profits, and not all of them are profitable in any given year. Shareholders of the profitable corporations receive dividends; those of less profitable corporations may not. Only a few corporations make sizeable profits, so only a minority of shareholders receive significant dividends. And in most cases, only people born on or before December 18, 1971, are shareholders.

As UAA anthropology professor Dr. Phyllis Fast notes:
ANCSA has had a tremendous and ongoing impact on Alaska Native identity with its cutoff date of birth (December 18, 1971) for inclusion into its provisions. All Alaska Natives born after that date were expected to assimilate into the mainstream population and/or inherit ANCSA shares from their parents and grandparents. In cultures where huge families and longer lives have become the norm, many original shareholders are alive and well and continue to own their own shares. In 1987 (enacted in 1988), Congress passed the "1991 Amendments" to allow, among other things, each of the twelve regional ANCSA corporations to vote to include descendants as shareholders. Of the twelve regional corporations, four (Arctic Slope Regional Corporation, NANA, Doyon Limited, and in 2007, Sealaska) have voted to grant descendants (commonly known as "afterborns") new shares. Each of these corporations has implemented different strategies to decide if or how to make the process work, and each of their solutions has resulted in differing notions of inclusion.[6]

What do Alaska Native people think of ANCSA?

Some Alaska Native people view ANCSA as a very positive step forward for Alaska Native peoples in terms of economic empowerment, while others see it as a necessary compromise to prevent all-out loss of traditional lands.

On the positive side, some see ANCSA as the first settlement in America based on self-determination for Native groups. Where earlier assimilation policies denigrated indigenous affiliations, ANCSA has opened the doors to learning about individual heritage, history, and culture. It has provided a focal point for increasing a common sense of Alaska Native identity and has resulted in a renaissance of culture, reflected today in the many Alaska Native cultural events around the state and the revival of interest in preserving Alaska Native languages. In addition, the economic and political power resulting from the creation of Alaska Native corporations has made a great many things possible in Alaska that indigenous nations in the Lower 48 have as yet been unable to achieve.

Others, however, agree with the sentiments expressed by Alaska Native activists Bigjim and Adler in "Letters to Howard"—that ANCSA was simply another step in a long history of the United States government's efforts to assimilate Native peoples and, ultimately, destroy their distinct cultures. "With the President's signature on the settlement act, the relationship between the Native peoples of Alaska and the land was completely transformed..." note Bigjim and Adler. "Native Alaskans whose earlier use and occupancy had made them co-owners of shared land, now became shareholders in corporate-owned land."[7] Other critics argue that ANCSA's use of the corporate form requires Alaska's Native peoples to embrace class relationships and values—such as profit-making from the "development of resources," placing a monetary value on land, and individual ownership of camphouses—that dangerously skew the more holistic relationships between the people and the land, as well as between the people and their communities, embodied by traditional Alaska Native cultures.

Despite its intent to resolve important issues, ANCSA remains a topic of debate more than three decades after its passage—an indication of the fundamental place that land and all it stands for continue to have for Alaska's Native peoples.

---

1. Some Native groups take issue with this theory and point to their own creation/origin stories which suggest other possible explanations and timeframes for their longstanding occupancy. The oldest subsistence sites discovered are at least ten thousand years old. Older sites may have disappeared under coastal waters.

2–5. Jones, Richard S. "Alaska Native Claims Settlement Act of 1971 (Public Law 92-203): History and Analysis Together with Subsequent Amendments," Report No. 81-127 GOV, June 1, 1981. www.alaskool.org/projects/ANCSA/reports/rsjones1981/ANCSA_History71.htm#Introduction\

6. Fast, Phyllis. "Alaska Native Language, Culture and Identity," 2008.

7. Alaska Native Heritage Center, Alaska Native Cultural Workshop Series packet, 2007.

Entrance to Arctic Slope Regional Corporation (ASRC) building, Anchorage, Alaska.

"Thus, investment and land use decisions of the Native corporations must reflect the concerns of their shareholders, even though many of these concerns are social rather than business. Native shareholders want more than just a dividend. They want protection of the subsistence lifestyle, jobs, access to their corporate leaders, enhancement of their culture, and other considerations which seldom, if ever, are discussed in the board rooms of profit-making corporations."

John Shively

READINGS

Please visit our web site at
**http://www.uaa.alaska.edu/books-of-the-year/
year08-09/supplemental_readings.cfm**
for a variety of supplemental readings

Online Readings

Arnold, Robert. *Alaska Native Land Claims.* Anchorage: Alaska Native Foundation, 1978.
   Though dated, a key text about the history and politics of the Native land claims in Alaska.

Bigjim, Frederick Seagayuk and James Ito-Adler. *Letters to Howard: An Interpretation of the
Alaska Native Land Claims.* Anchorage: Alaska Methodist University Press, 1974.
   Early concerns about the Alaska Native Claims Settlement Act written as letters to the editor from
   fictional characters.

Fast, Phyllis. "A Legacy of Sharing." *Sakuuktugut: Alaska Native Corporations.* Alexandra J.
McClahanan, ed. Anchorage: CIRI Foundation, 2006.
   Discusses how the traditional Native value of sharing has been incorporated into modern practices
   of Alaska Native corporations.

Hall, Joelle et al. "Wooch Yayi: Woven Together—Alaska Native Corporations 2005 Economic Data:
A Look at the 13 Regional Native Corporations and Three Native Village Corporations." Anchorage:
ANCSA Regional Corporation Presidents and CEOs, 2007.

Hensley, William L. Iggiagruk. "What Rights to Land Have the Alaska Natives?" May 2001.
   Paper written by Iñupiaq land claims leader Willie Hensley as a graduate student in a UA
   Constitutional Law class in 1966. Researching and writing this paper sparked Hensley's lifetime
   activism on behalf of Native peoples and their lands and cultures.

LitSite Alaska. ANCSA at 30. http://www.litsite.org/index.cfm?section=history-and-
culture&page=ANCSA-at-30
   Interviews with Native and non-Native leaders and citizens thirty years after the passage of the
   Alaska Native Claims Settlement Act.

Mallott, Byron. "One Day in the Life of a Native Chief Executive." In *Alaska Native News* 2 (October
1985):22.
   Tlingit leader Byron Mallott describes an ordinary day as the CEO of an Alaska Native corporation,
   with activities both similar to and distinct from non-Native corporations.

Mallott, Byron. "Unfinished Business: The Alaska Native Claims Settlement Act." LitSite Alaska. http://www.litsite.org.

> Tlingit leader and former president and CEO of First Alaskans Foundation wrestles with the role of ANCSA and Native corporations in a Native-centered vision for the future.

Hard Copy Readings

Berger, Thomas. *Village Journey: The Report of the Alaska Native Review Commission.* New York: Hill & Wang, 1985.

Case, David S., and David A. Voluck. *Alaska Natives and American Laws.* Fairbanks: University of Alaska Press, 2002.

> Major work on the legal status of Alaska Native peoples.
> Recommended excerpt:
> ■ Chapter 2, "Aboriginal Title."

Fitzgerald, Joseph H., David M. Hickok, Robert D. Arnold, and Esther C. Wunnicke. *Alaska Natives and the Land.* Federal Field Committee for Development Planning. Anchorage, United States Government Printing Office, 1968.

> Recommended excerpt:
> ■ "The Land Issue."

McClanahan, Alexandra J. *Growing up Native in Alaska.* Fairbanks: Todd Communications, 2001.

> Interviews with twenty seven young Alaska Native leaders about their lives, their futures, the impact of the Alaska Native Claims Settlement Act, and how they are "finding innovative and creative ways to live in two worlds." This was a UAA/APU Book of the Year for 2008–2009.

McClanahan, Alexandra J. *Sakuuktugut: Alaska Native Corporations.* Anchorage: CIRI Foundation, 2006.

> Book by noted CIRI historian that places Alaska Native corporations in the context of Alaska's history, economic and social issues, and explains why Native leaders and corporation shareholders struggle daily with the tension between focusing on bottom-line success and honoring traditional values and preserving cultures. The title is the Iñupiaq word for "we are working incredibly hard."

Morgan, Lael. *Art and Eskimo Power: The Life and Times of Alaskan Howard Rock.* Fairbanks: Epicenter Press, 1988.

> Founding editor of the only statewide Alaska Native newspaper, Howard Rock also played a vital part in pressing for Alaska Native claims to traditional land.

Other Resources

Alaska Department of Education. "ANCSA: Caught in the Act: The Alaska Native Claims Settlement Act." Six-part short video series. Alaska Native Foundation, 1987.

> http://www.ankn.uaf.edu/curriculum/ANCSA/caught.html

Clark James Mishler

Subsistence hunter Peter Spein retrieves duck from small pond near Kwethluk.

Subsistence and Relationship to Land, Waters, and Wildlife

Do Alaska's Native peoples want subsistence hunting and fishing rights that are different from non-Natives?

Why are the land and waters so important to Native cultures?

What do the phrases "traditional ways of knowing" or "traditional knowledge and wisdom" mean?

How is climate change affecting Native communities?

Do some Native corporations and organizations support drilling, mining, and logging on their lands?

"The Indian people used every part of every animal they killed. The skins were tanned and made into clothing. The bones were made into spear and arrowheads, needles, knives, spoons and ornaments. The sinew was used for thread to sew with. Some of the skin before it was tanned was made into rawhide (rope) of every size. The large intestines were used to store oil or moose fat. The horns of the moose or caribou were used to make bowls or large spoons....All animals that were killed were treated with much respect."

Alberta Stephan

Do Alaska's Native peoples want subsistence hunting and fishing rights that are different from non-Natives?

"Subsistence" is the term most often used to describe a way of life that Alaska's Native peoples have lived for thousands of years (and the way all cultures lived prior to the development of agriculture). It is a way of life in which everything—the economy, people's relationships to one another, philosophy, spirituality, science, technology, health care, artistic expression, education, jokes, ideas about gender and sexuality, entertainment, the creation of tools, shelter, and clothing is intimately tied to the land and the waters upon which the people depend for sustenance.

The subsistence activities—hunting (both land and sea mammals), fishing, berry-picking, and harvesting wild plants and shellfish—not only allow Alaska Native families to feed and clothe their families, but also provide the center for their entire lives and communities. From "time immemorial" (as the elders say), Alaska Native groups have provided for themselves directly from the land and sea, not through a cash economy, but through their own hard work and ingenuity. They traded for, or created by hand, all the things they needed to survive—parkas, boats, fishing nets, dwellings, footwear, eating utensils, blankets—in some of the harshest natural environments in the world.[1]

"Our culture's real rich as far as whaling goes. There's so much respect for the bowhead whale. Basically, that's what our community's based around. What I've learned—what I grew up with and maintained—is sharing. You don't get the whale. It comes to you. That's what I've been taught."

Rex Rock

It wasn't until the twentieth century—with the arrival of so many migrants to Alaska—that the cash economy, an exploding non-Native population, industrial technologies, and local, national, and international business interests began to seriously impact this age-old way of life.[2] Many Alaska Native communities have continued to adapt to their environment by integrating new technologies (snowmobiles, outboard motors) into their traditional subsistence activities. Many survive by continuing to hunt and fish for their livelihoods, while also trying to secure enough cash to afford the extremely costly fuel and foods that are now part of village life.[3] The average Alaska Native per capita consumption of wild foods is 375 pounds per year—about one pound per day.[4] According to a 1990 study by the Alaska Department of Labor, over 50 percent of rural Native households make less than $20,000 per year.[5] Many rural Alaska Native citizens depend upon wild foods to keep them from malnutrition and hunger. And sharing with others who cannot participate in subsistence activities—elders, the ill, young children—is a central value of Native cultures. Others have been forced to give up subsistence activities in whole or in part and to migrate to Alaska's urban centers in order to find jobs in the cash economy—a wrenching change. In recent times, more and more Alaska Native people are being born and raised entirely in urban settings without much exposure to the traditional subsistence ways of their parents or grandparents.

The Alaska Native subsistence way of life is central to individual and community health and well-being and to the viability of indigenous cultures. [6] Traditionally, Alaska Native peoples derive their food, nutrition, ethics and values of stewardship, languages, codes of conduct, stories, songs, dances, ceremonies, rites of passage, history, and sense of place and spirituality from the lands, waters, fish, and wildlife they have depended on for millennia. Alaska Native communities would prefer much stronger legal protection for this way of life, including legal definitions not simplistically tied to economic or physical needs. However, most of the Alaska Native leadership today believes that, given mainstream ignorance about the importance and meaning of subsistence to Alaska Native peoples, they are unlikely to secure stronger definitions in Congress in the foreseeable future.

The government definitions of subsistence involve the use of, and access to, sources of wild foods. The Alaska National Interest Land Conservation Act (ANILCA) passed by Congress in 1980 includes federal recognition of a "rural preference" for subsistence hunting and fishing and provisions for rural priority to "subsistence resources in times of scarcity."

Vera Spein at her fish camp near Kwethluk.

The use of the term "rural preference" rather than "Alaska Native preference," was an attempt to skirt the potential legal issue of allocating public resources to a specific ethnic group, despite widespread acknowledgement that Alaska's Native peoples have depended upon, and continue to depend upon, fish, wildlife, and habitat in Alaska for at least ten thousand years. [7] According to the Alaska Department of Fish and Game: "Both Alaska Natives and non-Natives may hunt and fish for subsistence if they live in rural areas. Currently, more than half of the people who qualify for subsistence are non-Natives."[8]

Even given this broader language and the inclusion of non-Natives, certain sport and commercial hunting and fishing interests have consistently, and so far unsuccessfully, attempted legal challenges to the language. These groups hope to eliminate "rural preference," arguing that such language is either a disguise for an ethnic-based distribution of "public resources" or violates United States constitutional provisions for protection of "individuals." [9] However, while commercial fisheries take nearly 97 percent of the total weight of fish and wildlife harvested in Alaska (roughly two billion pounds), rural subsistence activities account for only forty-five million pounds, or just 2 percent. Sports fishing and hunting account for 1 percent of the total harvest (approximately eighteen billion pounds).[10]

Given this tiny percentage of the harvest by Native and non-Native subsistence hunters combined, Alaska Native citizens have a difficult time understanding why these constituencies would try to deny protection for them to continue to feed their families and engage in the activities that are central to their physical, economic, cultural and spiritual well-being—activities without which Native cultural traditions will die.

---

1. Berger, Thomas R. *Village Journey*. New York: Hill and Wang, 1985.
    Key text about the effects of the Alaska Native Claims Settlement Act on Alaska Native villages which includes extensive quotes from Alaska Native people throughout Alaska.
2. Wolfe, Robert J., and Robert J. Walker. "Subsistence Economies in Alaska: Productivity, Geography, and Development Impacts." *Arctic Anthropology* 24, no. 2 (1987):56–81.
3. Berger, Thomas R. *Village Journey*. New York: Hill and Wang, 1985.
4. Alaska Department of Fish and Game, 2000. http://www.subsistence.adfg.state.ak.us/download/subupd00.pdf .
5. Dubbs, Patrick J. "Small Alaska Native Villages: Are They Worth Saving?" December 2, 1992 paper to the 91st Annual Meeting of the American Anthropological Association. http://www.ankn.uaf.edu/curriculum/Articles/PatrickDubbs/akvillages.html
6. Berger, Thomas R. *Village Journey*. New York: Hill and Wang, 1985.
    Tundra Times Special Subsistence Issue 25, no. 18. (June 19, 1996).
    Merculieff, Ilarion "Larry." Alaska Native Fish, Wildlife, Habitat, and Environment Summit Final Report. Anchorage: RurAL CAP, 2001.
7. Case, David S. "Subsistence and Self-Determination: Can Alaska Natives Have a More Effective Voice?" *University of Colorado Law Review* 60, no. 4 (1992):1009–35.
    Kancewick, Mary, and Eric Smith. "Subsistence in Alaska: Towards a Native Priority." *UMKC Law Review* 59, no. 3 (1991):645–677.
8. Alaska Department of Fish and Game Frequently Asked Questions about Subsistence by Robert Wolfe
    http://www.subsistence.adfg.state.ak.us/geninfo/about/subfaq.cfm
9. Case, David S. "Subsistence and Self-Determination: Can Alaska Natives Have a More Effective Voice?" *University of Colorado Law Review*. 60, no. 4 (1992):1009–35.
    Kancewick, Mary, and Eric Smith. "Subsistence in Alaska: Towards a Native Priority." *UMKC Law Review* 59, no. 3 (1991):645–677.
10. Alaska Department of Fish and Game, Division of Subsistence, *Subsistence in Alaska: A Year 2000 Update*
    http://www.subsistence.adfg.state.ak.us/download/subupd00.pdf.

Why are the land and waters so important to Native cultures?

For nearly ten thousand years, Alaska's Native peoples have occupied much of the usable lands (lakes, rivers, and coastal areas) in Alaska. Given that these lands and waters were and are the sources of community, family, and individual sustenance, as well as the source of materials for their arts, crafts, and technologies, Alaska Native peoples understand that they would not exist as peoples, communities, and cultures without them. For these reasons, and for reasons related to spirituality and the Alaska Native cosmologies involving intimate connection with creation, Alaska Native peoples have exercised wise stewardship and passed along their knowledge and wisdom about the land, waters, and wildlife to each new generation. The cultural practices and cosmologies of Alaska Native peoples were so successful that when Europeans first arrived in Alaska, they found the land and waters to be completely pristine, teeming with fish and wildlife.

The land provides berries, vegetation used for food and medicine, wood for lighting fires and for building materials, and wildlife critical to the viability of all Alaska Native cultures and communities. The waters are habitat for fish, fish eggs, ducks, sea vegetables, and marine mammals—all sources of food that provide sustenance for Alaska Native families—and provide the surface for long-distance travel by boat (summer) or, in recent times, snowmachine (winter).

Land and water, combined with sunlight, are the source of all things used by all people on the planet to survive and thrive. Indigenous cultures are, perhaps, more highly aware of their importance than many other modern societies because they have lived directly from the land, water, and wildlife for tens of thousands of years, rather than engaging in agricultural or industrial economies.

"I come from a family of reindeer herders. Reindeer husbandry is all about balance between current needs (for food and sustenance) and future growth opportunities (for a larger herd beyond just personal needs). To be a successful reindeer herder, you need both. You need to eat, but you need to save some of your animals to grow your herd. In life and in business, we must be careful stewards of our resources and strive to achieve this balance."

Margaret L. Brown

Gladys Johnson, formerly of Hooper Bay, spends many days in Anchorage's Arctic Valley filling her bucket (and her freezer) with the annual bounty of blueberries and blackberries.

What do the phrases "traditional ways of knowing" or "traditional knowledge and wisdom" mean?

"Traditional ways of knowing" and "traditional knowledge and wisdom" are western terms that have evolved out of a gradual awareness on the part of western scientists and researchers that Alaska's Native peoples are experts about their environments and embody worldviews critical to the human future. To define these terms in the way Alaska Native cultures traditionally understand them would be to introduce the reader to a completely different way of perceiving and living in the world.

Because of a long history of ignorance and racism, the knowledge and wisdom derived from thousands of years of direct experience with, dependence upon, observation of, and interaction with the natural world by Alaska Native communities was historically ignored, dismissed, or marginalized. Over the past few decades, scientists and researchers in higher education and government have begun to recognize the value of the information, knowledge, and holistic worldview developed by Alaska Native cultures. Indeed, many of these western institutions have slowly begun to realize that some of the limitations of western approaches—such as a tendency to compartmentalize knowledge and expertise—can be ameliorated by Native approaches, and that some of the cutting edge developments in western science (such as complex systems and chaos theory) have preexisting parallels in Native ways of thinking.

"A number of years ago a Native Elder was telling me something was happening. The ice was changing. The changes would have a tremendous impact on subsistence and on the way people lived. NOAA has spent millions of dollars to come to the same conclusion. It took time for science to catch up with what the Elders were telling us. We need to look more at the traditional knowledge embodied in our Elders."

Nelson Angapak

Traditional knowledge and wisdom involves a qualitative understanding of (1) how cultures are sustained in extreme climates; (2) how, when, and where to access subsistence foods; (3) daily and seasonal weather patterns; (4) sustainable food harvesting techniques and strategies; (5) wildlife biology and behavior patterns; (6) how to adapt to climactic changes; (7) complex natural interrelationships; (8) abnormal natural phenomena in the context of long time periods; and (9) qualitative historical knowledge and information of the natural world.

Because their lives have depended on the natural world for at least ten thousand years, Alaska's Native peoples have traditionally been trained to observe the subtlest changes in wildlife and environment, and are therefore often aware of trends and anomalies in their regions far in advance of the western scientific community. No other peoples in the world, and no science, can replicate what Alaska Native elders and cultures know and understand about their immediate environments and the wildlife that breed in their areas. "Indigenous people…have their own classification systems and versions of meteorology, physics, chemistry, earth science, astronomy, botany, pharmacology, psychology (knowing one's inner world), and the sacred."[1] This traditional knowledge and wisdom is a highly sophisticated holistic science that evolved through methodical cultural processes of the transfer of knowledge and wisdom through hundreds of generations, learning and applying a holistic way of knowing, collective information sharing, traditional spirituality, and guidance from elders.

It is important to note that Native elders only use the term "traditional knowledge" in conjunction with the term "wisdom": "traditional knowledge and wisdom." From the perspective of the elders, it is the accumulation of vast amounts of knowledge without a corresponding development of wisdom that has brought humanity to the brink of destruction. According to elders, human beings strive for information and knowledge, when what is needed even more is wisdom—the willingness to delve into our hearts and minds and put right what is askew in the human family. Environmental degradation, strife, and resource conflicts will not be solved unless these deeper issues are understood and addressed more profoundly.

How is climate change affecting Alaska's Native communities?

As public policy-makers increasingly acknowledge, Alaska is at "ground zero" for the effects of climate change. However, few have acknowledged that Alaska's Native peoples in rural communities are at the center of "ground zero." The fates of fish, wildlife, and Alaska Native cultures and communities are intimately connected.

Today, sea ice in Alaska waters arrives later, recedes earlier, and is thinner than ever recorded in human history. These conditions affect the survival of all ice-dependent mammals such as seals, walruses, and polar bears, all of which are key sources of protein and fat which allow many Alaska Native communities to survive through the harsh northern winters. Changes in sea temperatures and weather systems have been confirmed as a primary factor in the catastrophic declines of Steller sea lions, northern fur seals, ducks, crabs, and fishes connected to the Bering Sea adjacent to southwestern Alaska. These species have provided basic dietary staples for Native peoples in that region for thousands of years. Migratory patterns of ducks, moose, reindeer, and caribou are dramatically changing, which can result in hunger for families and communities as hunters come home empty-handed.

Water levels in lakes, streams, and rivers all across Alaska have significantly changed. Alaska Native elders fear that changing river water levels—and the resulting increase in water temperatures—will adversely affect salmon health and reproduction, once again having a huge negative impact on Native diets. Beaver are now proliferating in rivers throughout Alaska, perhaps due to changes in vegetation, causing more problems with river water levels due to the effects of beaver dams. Many animals are becoming food stressed due to changes in vegetation. Weather conditions are less predictable and more intense than ever in living memory, threatening hunter and traveler safety.

Several Alaska Native communities in Northwestern Alaska are facing the potential destruction of their villages by erosion from storm-driven waves. These waves are higher than ever before due to increased storm intensities fueled by changes in the global climate. Historically, these villages were protected by sea ice that prevented encroachment of waves on the shorelines. In recent times, however, ice no longer protects them because it, too, has been impacted by rising global temperatures.

Scientific institutions and governmental policy-makers are responding to the emergencies experienced by these coastal communities. However, they have yet to proactively approach the challenge of protecting all rural Native communities—and the Native cultures which depend upon subsistence for physical, economic, cultural, and spiritual survival—in a systematic, critical way. Alaska Native leaders call upon them to do so now, before it is too late.

"When you don't hear the animals in the woods something is wrong. These are . . . some of the changes that we have seen in Huslia, Alaska. In my community, fire has become less predictable. It gets too hot and too dry in our area now. There is little we can do under these conditions to protect the community. Fires blew through the buffers we have built around the community. Native Elders said it burned less severely before. The plants are confused now. Flowers bloom when they shouldn't. There is no permafrost. In September, when we used to have snow, it now rains. There are higher river levels as well that have led to more erosion. We have to move our possessions far from the riverbank. To practice the subsistence way of life we rely on healthy salmon runs. For many years now these runs aren't healthy. The water is too warm. We may have to make new fishing rules that work for all of us. Maybe we will have to look at agriculture. I can't raise animals because these are my ancestors. Elders don't want to move from the river. The natural cycles are out of place. We need to teach our children what is important. What are the climate change indicators to look at?"

Orville Huntington

Do some Native corporations support drilling, mining, and logging on their lands?

Editor's note: Land and resource issues can be highly charged in Alaska. This seemingly simple question is tied to a host of highly complex issues involving not only economic development but, more fundamentally, questions of governance—who gets to make decisions and exercise authority. In a departure from previous questions in this book, we asked two individuals to describe their personal reactions to the question and to provide responses from their own experiences. They are joined in this new edition by a third perspective from an individual who shares some of their concerns while disagreeing with others. These three essays make it clear that a responsible discussion of this question requires an understanding of the unique history, purpose, structure, challenges, and opportunities of Alaska Native corporations. We encourage readers to explore other perspectives on this important question as well.

One Response: A Broad Perspective

By Paul Ongtooguk

Paul Ongtooguk, an Iñupiaq from Northwest Alaska, is an assistant professor of education at UAA. He is an educator who has also been involved in decision-making at the tribal (Kotzebue IRA) level.

Do Alaska Native corporations support mining, logging, and drilling? As an Alaska Native, when I hear this question, my first response is to brace myself for a difficult conversation. Frequently, those asking the question are non-Natives who are unfamiliar with the structure and economic missions of the Alaska Native regional corporations. Typically the questioner hopes that the answer is "No."

However, the honest response to the question is simply to say, "Yes, some Alaska Native corporations do support mining, some support logging, and others support drilling for natural gas and oil." That is an accurate answer and can be checked through any number of public records. Still, simply acknowledging that these activities occur is not a blank check of support for any and all activities, but a consideration of this kind of development.

For many, however, the answer to this question is already known, and the real intent behind the conversation is to try to determine why some Native corporations support these activities. At this point, the framework for the question matters as much as the question itself. Fundamentally and most directly, the answer relates to the economic mission of the Alaska

Native corporations. Considered more indirectly, however, the question is often framed from an ecological and conservationist perspective that tends to oppose mineral, subsurface, and other resource development anywhere in Alaska.

First, the direct answer. Alaska Native corporations are divided into for-profit and nonprofit corporations. The nonprofit corporations include Alaska Native health corporations, Heritage centers, and educational programs. They were designed by Alaska Native leaders and operate on behalf of Alaska Native tribal governments to combine their efforts and provide social, cultural, and educational services and programs for their tribal citizens. Other Alaska Native nonprofit corporations have other goals and purposes.

Alaska Native for-profit corporations, created by an act of Congress through the Alaska Native Claims Settlement Act (ANCSA) of 1971, hold a unique state-chartered status. The ANCSA corporations were chartered to select and take title to the lands kept by Alaska Native peoples under ANCSA, and to receive and invest the money from other lands to which claims had been dropped. At the time they were formed, the village corporations had the option of becoming either for-profit or nonprofit entities and, in an historic decision, all chose to become for-profit corporations.

This point (little noted at the time), has had great consequence since. In brief, these for-profit corporations generate profits that are distributed to corporation shareholder-members. Economically, they function in a similar manner to other western corporations, and management and members are generally happy whenever money is made. Native corporations, however, are also distinct in that their history is cultural (rather than economic). Again in brief, the relationship of Native corporations to their history and culture means that they cannot be understood, analyzed, or explained in strictly economic terms; they are, rather, a complicated tangle of economics, cultural conservation, and history.

"ANCSA corporations currently control all remaining Alaska Native lands and are making enormous economic and social decisions that will affect the future of all Alaska Native lands, waters, and people. "

Paul Ongtooguk

Now to consider the question from the more indirect perspective. The people who ask this question are, in my experience, almost always non-Natives whose vision of Alaska is that of a vast land that should be preserved in a natural ("wilderness") state in perpetuity. To most of them, "wilderness" does not include human occupation or use. The questioners tend to be conservationists, opposed to mining, logging, or drilling in Alaska in general. Their view of Alaska Native peoples tends to be narrowed to their understanding of Natives as historically careful and judicious stewards of the land, and they therefore believe that Alaska Native peoples are natural allies for the non-Native conservationist agenda. This view ignores, however, the realities of modern life that all segments of the Alaska population face as they grapple with technology, economics, and quality of life issues. It also ignores the historical record which has left Alaska Native peoples amongst the poorest groups in the nation.

I am assuming—perhaps generously—that most conservationists are not simply NIMBYs (Not In My Backyarders) on a statewide or even national scale. They don't endorse the use of the products of these activities (metals, wood products, fuel) while having someone else—perhaps in a third world country—live with the consequences. Instead they are expressing a concern about the manner or location in which a particular development project is occurring. In my opinion, any for-profit corporation with significant mineral or timber resources has a fair right to ask those who challenge them for examples of places or practices in which they have supported, or would be willing to support, a profitable development project. Normally the conversation gets pretty quiet at that point. Many conservationists fail to offer viable economic alternatives to current options, yet maintain lifestyles dependent upon the activities to which they object.

"Those involved in Native issues wrestle with the huge challenge of how to help lift the economic boats of Alaska's Native peoples while simultaneously protecting the cultures, lands, and waters of our peoples."

Paul Ongtooguk

Some Alaska Native people ask versions of this question as well, but they are most often coming from a very different place than non-Native questioners. ANCSA corporations currently control all remaining Alaska Native lands and are making enormous economic and social decisions that will affect the future of all Alaska Native lands, waters, and people. Particularly, given that few Alaska Native people born after December 18, 1971 have a role in corporate decisions, we should raise the question of how to give all Alaska Native peoples a strong voice in those decisions. Who should have the final say about development, land use, and investments based on ANCSA lands and monies? Corporate Boards of Directors? Shareholders? Alaska Native citizens, including non-shareholders? Tribal governments?

I believe there needs to be a reliable way for revitalized regional tribal governments to have a role in overseeing and giving a broader voice for Alaska Native peoples regarding economic development decisions affecting our lands and futures. Tribal governments are imperfect vehicles, but regional tribal governments (as opposed to village governments, which tend to have too local a focus) could serve as an important counterbalance to corporate power when and if that counterbalance is required. When an ANCSA corporation proposes a new use for ANCSA lands and waters, the regional Alaska Native tribal governments should have an explicit responsibility to oversee a vote by enrolled Alaska Native citizens to determine the issue. Legislation should give shareholders and descendants of shareholders the opportunity to vote whenever a corporation proposes an economic development project that will have a significant impact on a particular region's lands and waters.

There may be other, and better, solutions. This is a vital question to address within the Alaska Native communities as we face an uncertain future. What is clear to me is that the people for whom these lands and waters have been and continue to be homelands from time immemorial should have first say about how to protect this vital inheritance. Most of the problems we experience in our Alaska Native communities stem from the fact that we have not had—and still do not have—enough control over our own political, economic, cultural, and social destiny. I believe most of the answers to our challenges will come when large numbers of Alaska Native people are able to do more than offer commentary (duly noted and then usually ignored) with respect to the decisions that affect our lands and futures.

I am an Alaska Native and a shareholder in a corporation with a history of marginal management. To me, it seems desirable when a for-profit Native corporation tries to make a profit for its shareholders. Ideally, as with all corporations, it should do so within the limits of good stewardship of the earth. Corporate managers need to keep the well-being of the next generation, as well as of the next shareholder meeting, in mind (not as common a practice as one would hope).

If this is what the questioners are trying to address, then Native people welcome them into the fray of the dilemmas faced by ANCSA corporations today. Those involved in Native issues wrestle with the huge challenge of how to help lift the economic boats of Alaska's Native peoples while simultaneously protecting the cultures, lands, and waters of our peoples. If the questioners are committed to both goals as well, we welcome the discussion. However, if they wish us to maintain pristine lands and waters without being equally concerned with our cultural, social, and economic well-being, it seems to me that they are asking us to do something unacceptable—to sacrifice our relationship to and use of our lands and waters on behalf of non-Natives who can, in the future, afford to fly in and enjoy what would then be our former homelands.

ANCSA corporations try to achieve both of these goals in the face of some unique conditions. Thrown into the mix of these goals is the relatively new nature of Native corporations in Alaska, and the continued lack of enough Alaska Native professionals at all levels of these organizations. (In part, this lack derives from the historical tendency of educators to view Alaska Native people merely as sources of unskilled or entry-level labor throughout most of the educational history of Alaska.) Consider, too, that some of the newly minted Alaska Native professionals may lack any sense of the history and nature of the unique role and purposes of these Native corporations. I am not aware of any MBA programs, including those at the University of Alaska, that offer any real understanding of the structure, mission, or histories of Native corporations as a part of their programs. This is especially surprising given that ANCSA corporations have dramatically changed the economic landscape of Alaska. Toss in the fact that Alaska Native shareholders now make up less than half of the

Alaska Native people today and things become even more volatile, both socially and organizationally. Now try to make a profit. Given all these factors, it would seem irresponsible for ANCSA corporations not to consider mineral resources, oil, gas, and timber as potential sources of profit.

From my perspective, oil development on land has been far less harmful than oil development offshore. The major disasters concerning oil have been off the coasts of the world—Spain, South Africa, France, the Gulf of Mexico, Southern California, and Ireland, to name a few. Given that, I am surprised that conservationist efforts in Alaska have not been more focused on offshore oil production rather than proposals for development on land, especially the small fraction of lands owned by Alaska Natives. It would seem like an environmental bargain to trade offshore leases for limited onshore exploration and development. This position neatly offends both the oil companies and the conservationists—not an uncommon situation when interests differ from both camps at times.

"The Alaska Native Claims Settlement Act was a giant act of compromise on the part of Alaska's Native peoples; we had to make huge sacrifices of our lands in order to arrive at any kind of a settlement."

Paul Ongtooguk

As an Alaska Native, I can offer a personal view on the question as well. Some see ANCSA corporation economic development projects as being at odds with the responsible stewardship of these lands. I agree that within the ANCSA corporations there is a built-in tension between profitability and stewardship goals. Occasionally, some of the ANCSA corporations (like many non-Native corporations) have seemingly been driven more by short-term bonuses and quarterly profit reports, rather than by a "marathon awareness" that these ANCSA lands are also the last lands future Alaska Native generations might inherit. In this regard, I share some of the conservationists' concerns, as do many other Alaska Native people.

However, I am also reminded by history that many of the non-Native conservation organizations that commonly oppose ANCSA corporation resource development projects also opposed the Alaska Native effort to obtain title to some of our traditional lands through ANCSA. The Alaska Native Claims Settlement Act was a giant act of compromise on the part of Alaska's Native peoples; we had to make huge sacrifices of our lands in order to arrive at any kind of a settlement. The price of support from the major conservation organizations was section 17(d)2 of ANCSA. This provision promised that up to eight-five million acres of Alaska would be considered for further protection as parks, preserves, refuges, etc. These lands had historically been Native lands. Native corporations were allowed to keep only forty-four million acres. In effect, the much more powerful conservationist lobby won twice the land for its purposes than Alaska Native peoples did in our own land claims settlement. This fact comes to mind when conservationists criticize what Native corporations do to try to provide economic benefits for their shareholders on the lands left to them, many of which are set aside for subsistence purposes.

Indeed, over the decade following the passage of ANCSA, conservationist organizations went on a "shopping spree" for additional lands, visiting many parts of Alaska normally considered home only by Alaska Native peoples. For a great snapshot of this time, if a sympathetic one for the conservationist, read John McPhee's bestselling book *Coming into the Country*. As it turns out, like many shoppers, the conservationists ended up wanting more than they had first thought they would, and so the Alaska National Interest Land Conservation Act of 1980 (ANILCA) was born—the step child of ANCSA. Among other things, ANILCA enlarged the amount of land set aside for protection, creating over 100 million acres of conservation lands. This act almost immediately turned many Alaska Native lands into "in-holdings" surrounded by newly minted parks, monuments, etc. In fact, the term is misleading; if we consider who was here first, the ANILCA creations are actually "out-holdings."

What does all this have to do with the original question? I am hoping to provide a larger framework for a responsible discussion of ANCSA economic development activities. Over three hundred million acres of Native lands were taken under ANCSA for which we received far less than fair market value. We also received title to less than half the amount of land that was set aside for conservation. These earlier generations of non-Native conservationists took much of our Alaska Native land, calming their collective conscience far too easily with the rhetoric that taking our lands was justified because these lands were now being put to better use. This paternalistic attitude describes federal policy towards indigenous peoples in the United States in general and in Alaska. The larger question of ANCSA corporations and their rightful or wrongful place in the future of Alaska Native people is beyond the scope of this essay. Whatever your position is about economic development on ANCSA lands, please keep in mind that unless you are an Alaska Native, you are talking about our last lands—not yours.

> "Over 300 million acres of Native lands were taken under ANCSA for which we received far less than fair market value. We also received title to less than half the amount of land that was set aside for conservation."
>
> Paul Ongtooguk

For further reading on this topic, I suggest the book *Alaska Native Land Claims* edited by Robert Arnold. Other materials can be found at www.alaskool.org, www.ANKN. org, the many websites of Native organizations, mining and development associations, the various branches of the federal and state governments related to Alaska lands, and the conservation organizations. Grappling with these issues will sometimes be overwhelming, but then so is Alaska.

Another Response: ANCSA and Economic Development

by Ilarion (Larry) Merculieff

Ilarion (Larry) Merculieff, an Aleut born and raised on St. Paul Island, has held a wide range of positions, including deputy director of the Alaska Native Science Commission, commissioner of the Alaska Department of Commerce and Economic Development, city manager of the city of St. Paul, CEO of the Tanadgusix Corporation of St. Paul Island, and chairman of the board of the Aleut Corporation.

I believe there is one significant area in which the ANCSA corporate structure and profit mandate is completely inappropriate, at least in its present form—and that is as it applies to use and development of traditional use lands selected by the regional corporations under ANCSA.

Although under U.S. laws ANCSA corporations are structured as any modern-day, for-profit corporations, they differ in that the lands they selected include large areas that have traditionally been, and continue to be, used by Alaska Native peoples for subsistence camps, subsistence hunting and fishing, berry picking, gathering of herbs and medicines, ceremonial and burial grounds, and sacred sites. They also differ from non-Native corporations in that non-Native corporations purchase lands for the sole purpose of development in order to generate profits and have shareholders who buy shares purely as financial investments.

ANCSA corporation shareholders are Alaska Native peoples with historical and ancestral ties, going back thousands of years, to the lands and waters owned by their corporations. ANCSA shareholders with roots to ancestral and traditional-use lands still depend on the natural conditions of their lands and waters for sustenance, spirituality, cultural viability, nutrition, and individual and community well-being. It is through hunting, fishing, and gathering that young people learn about the ethics and values of their cultures, including sharing, cooperation, reciprocity, and respect for the land, fish, and wildlife. Traditional activities on the lands and waters help strengthen family bonds and nurture relationships to others engaged in similar activities.

Experientially, hunters, fishers, and gatherers develop an intimate relationship with the land and waters. Knowledge gained from this intimacy is embedded within their traditional languages, and this relationship to the lands and waters makes the local, place-based language "alive." These facts place a special and profound moral, ethical, and cultural obligation upon ANCSA corporations to protect the pristine nature of these lands for the perpetuation of the cultures, ways of life, and well-being of the people they represent. Corporate laws and U.S. accounting systems do not place any value on well-being, subsistence ways of life, and cultural survival, and so there is no place for such things when corporations calculate the bottom line. If such important values were included in these laws and accounting systems, ANCSA corporations would be considered some of the richest corporations in America.

These special obligations of ANCSA corporations places them, vis-a-vis American corporate laws, in a schizophrenic situation. When I served as CEO of a village corporation in the 1980s, I searched for ways to protect and maintain traditionally valuable lands in their pristine state in perpetuity. Legal analysis showed that such action would be tantamount to "liquidating" corporate assets. Corporate laws (designed to protect shareholders) require the approval of a super majority of shareholders to take such action. As I discovered, the sad fact is that a significant number of the shareholders in most village or regional corporations no longer live on the lands or in the villages that form the basis for their corporations. Of those who live in cities, many are struggling to survive economically and need cold hard cash. Such a situation makes it extremely difficult, if not impossible, to secure the approval of a majority of shareholders in the protection of these lands.

Corporate laws create corporate responsibilities that can and do conflict with traditional, cultural, and social responsibilities. Because of these laws, any corporate asset can be taken by creditors if the corporation files for bankruptcy or is unable to pay creditors. Land, by definition, is an asset of ANCSA corporations. Any ANCSA corporate executive is fully aware that failure to create or maintain a solvent corporation could result not only in loss of traditionally valuable lands, but also in those lands ending up in the hands of creditors whose only concern is to recover losses from a bad debt or, worse yet, make profits off the lands. If the area lies within an organized borough under Alaska state laws, failure to pay taxes on the lands can also result in the

> "Corporate laws and U.S. accounting systems do not place any value on well-being, subsistence ways of life, and cultural survival, and so there is no place for such things when corporations calculate the 'bottom-line.' "
>
> Ilarion (Larry) Merculieff

lands being taken by the borough government. Furthermore, corporate laws are unequivocal in holding that boards of directors and chief executives are liable for any actions they take that are not in the "best interests" of the corporation. Such actions could result in being sued by any shareholder for "breach of fiduciary duty" or for not acting as any "reasonable" person would act under similar circumstances. By definition, under such laws, what is in the best interest of the corporation is profitability, among other things. Conceivably, failure to "develop" assets (even if the intent was to ensure cultural survival) could be construed as not acting in the best interests of the corporation, particularly if the corporation is, or is likely to be, struggling financially as a result. And the primary asset of most ANCSA corporations is their lands.

Given these scenarios, in conjunction with the primacy of American corporate laws, what can or should ANCSA corporations do when offered the prospect of making millions, or hundreds of millions, of dollars by developing their lands for oil, gas, mining, and timber cutting? Well, we can just look around to see the results of the corporate profit paradigms operating around the world: the fouling of our air and water; the warming of our planet from greenhouse gases; acidification of the world's oceans; the commoditization of plants and drinking water; deforestation; depletion of the nutrients in soils; elimination of genetic variation in industrialized agriculture; destruction of habitat; extinction of plants and animals; destruction of indigenous cultures; and the exploitation of earth's bounty to the point that, for the first time in human history, the life-sustaining systems of our planet are threatened. According to scientists around the globe, this paradigm may well spell the end of civilization as we know it.

> "I maintain that ANCSA corporations can model another way—perhaps a better way—where businesses work with nature to generate profits, rather than exploiting the natural world while giving nothing in return."
>
> Ilarion (Larry) Merculieff

I maintain that ANCSA corporations can model another way—perhaps a better way—where businesses work with nature to generate profits, rather than exploiting the natural world while giving nothing in return. We Native peoples should not adopt the ways of greed and power that are killing life-sustaining systems worldwide. ANCSA corporations should reject the destructive ways of western corporations and develop more culturally compatible ways of making profits. Doing so is not an easy task, for ANCSA corporations or any other businesses. It requires thinking outside the box to find creative solutions, including changing laws that give corporations more powers than individuals and communities. When an individual or organization outside an ANCSA region criticizes an ANCSA corporation for what it is doing, the critics should also step forward to help these corporations find other, less destructive but still profitable, options.

As the former Commissioner of the (then) Alaska Department of Commerce and Economic Development, city manager of St. Paul, CEO of the Tanadgusix Corporation of St. Paul Island, and chairman of the board of the Aleut Corporation, I am well aware of the economic and investment challenges and realities in rural Alaska. Rural communities have a relatively small human resource base to draw on; financing institutions are reluctant to provide loans for rural investments because they are considered "high risk"; the cost of doing business in rural Alaska is inordinately high compared to that in Alaska's urban centers; the cost of transportation, fuel, and construction are considerably higher than in urban Alaska; and investment opportunities in remote parts of Alaska are scarce. Nevertheless, it is possible to tackle these daunting issues. To develop non-destructive investment opportunities requires real creativity and critical strategic thinking.

When I served as president and CEO of the village corporation of St. Paul Island in the Pribilofs, we faced these challenges and more. St. Paul is eight hundred air miles west of Anchorage in the middle of the Bering Sea. It is accessible only by air, with supplies barged in two or three times a year. The village corporation committed to its shareholders that it would not engage in activities that would disrupt our way of life or the 1.2 million fur seals and 2.5 million seabirds that breed in the Pribilofs.

In order to live up to that commitment, we first conducted a visual "audit" of our cultural and other strengths through the use of video, utilizing the principle that we would focus our investments in our strong areas. With the help of two researchers, we completed a one-hour documentary on our cultural strengths and showed the first draft of this film to the community for review and approval. We then canvassed possible economic and investment activities that would utilize our cultural strengths. Prior to this time, our people had never engaged in private enterprise, with the exception of coffee shops. However, as a result of this audit, we developed a small eco-tour operation, a restaurant and hotel, construction contracting, and a commercial day-boat fishery.

Our people and wildlife were two community strengths identified in our audit. We started the hotel and restaurant because our people are friendly and have experience with cooking for large groups of people. The eco-tour endeavor included the following requirements: all tourists had to participate in an island orientation program upon arrival; all tours were conducted by a local guide; no dogs or firearms were allowed on the island; and independent camping was prohibited to minimize disruption to wildlife and protect habitat. Tourists stayed at our hotel and ate at our restaurant. This eco-tour enterprise has been touted statewide as a rural success story.

Another of the community's cultural strengths is that we know how and where to fish for halibut in small boats. The commercial day-boat operation started with two small demonstration halibut longline boats. Within four years, we had a fleet of boats catching almost a million pounds of halibut annually; our catch per unit effort exceeded, by a factor of four, that of the highly experienced halibut schooners out of Seattle and Kodiak.

We had other successful ventures. Using our newly-acquired experience in hotel and restaurant operations, we purchased a major hotel in Anchorage near the airport (now called the Anchorage West Coast International Inn) with favorable financing guarantees offered by the Bureau of Indian Affairs. The hotel has generated consistent profits every year of operation since it was purchased. We then pursued government funding for a port, contracted to provide various services, and leased land for fish and crab processing once the port was built. Since then, the corporation has succeeded in acquiring government contracts to test software for the military, and has become involved in several other innovative investments.

Given upcoming changes in the U.S. federal administration, regional and village corporations should position themselves to take advantage of favorable new directions and priorities, particularly in areas involving "bringing our jobs back to America." We are limited only by our creativity and imagination in terms of exploring viable and realistic opportunities. The following list offers food for thought on how Alaska Natives might harness some of these opportunities.

- If U.S. airlines contract with people in India to handle airline reservations, and bankcard companies use employees in other countries to field customer service calls, what stops Alaska Native peoples from being competitive and securing those contracts?
- Federal government agencies are required to set aside 5 percent of their contractual budgets to contract with minority companies. Village and regional corporations can develop investment consortia to aggressively pursue those kinds of contracts, in addition to the military contracts many have already taken advantage of.
- Billions, perhaps trillions, of dollars will eventually be budgeted to support global warming and climate change technologies, research, habitat restoration, and trade. Regional corporations in partnership with village corporations, and village corporation investment consortia, must position themselves to be active participants in these new investment opportunities.
- Given that we are immediate neighbors to Russia and the Far East, why are there only six or so foreign trade zones in Alaska? When I served as city manager for St. Paul, we succeeded in getting a Foreign Trade Zone designation for our community. If a small rural community in remote Alaska can secure such a designation (and there are only a little over 100 such zones in the entire U.S.), what is to stop rural regional hubs?
- Why should multinational companies control tourism in Alaska, when Alaska Natives have the cultures and many of the pristine lands in which visitors are keenly interested?
- Given the financial strengths of our corporations today, what prevents us from developing world-class strategic investment "think tanks" that engage some of the world's most forward-thinking, innovative visionaries to work with us?

Alaska Native corporations could also make profitable investments in alternative energy technologies. Rising power and fuel costs threaten the viability of many rural Alaska communities and cultures, as many people, especially the young and elderly, migrate to regional hubs and cities where the cost of living is more bearable. Remote villages have a critical need for business investments in alternative energy and energy efficiency technologies, and in making these technologies accessible to rural Alaskans. Technologies already exist to significantly improve the efficiency of trucks and power generators and could, with sufficient commitment and capitalization, be adapted to existing four wheelers and outboard motors. Use of wind power is expected to increase dramatically over the next decade. What better proving ground for wind power than Alaska's coastal and tundra communities? Native corporations could become leaders in such initiatives, simultaneously generating profits, lowering costs, and preserving cultures and communities.

There is a painful dearth of allies helping rural Alaska Native people address high rates of poverty and exorbitant costs of living, or supporting Alaska Native peoples in their fight to protect subsistence ways of living before Congress, the state legislature, and the Boards of Fish and Game (all of which continue to allow more and more sports hunting and fishing in rural areas). These subsistence ways of life are integral to the health and well-being of all Alaska Native communities, and certainly integral to their economies.

I vividly recall arguing that the North Pacific Fishery Management Council should recognize and honor Alaska Native peoples' subsistence rights to take only 1 percent of the annual halibut harvest (the other 99 percent of the halibut catch is taken by sports and commercial fishers). One member of the Council argued that, one day, Alaska Natives might want another 1 percent of the overall catch for subsistence purposes; on that basis, he stated that if there was a need for an additional 1 percent at some future time, it would not be taken out of the allowance for his sports fishing constituents. That argument was made just six years ago, and only Alaska Native peoples argued for their subsistence rights. No other group came forward in support of this modest demand.

What I describe is, unfortunately, not an isolated incident. Many similar stories play out across the state each month. But if Alaska Native corporations try to improve the lot of the people they represent by developing their lands, vocal critics tend to show up in force. I ask such groups to make a shift in their paradigms. Alaska Natives not only need opponents to some proposed developments, but also allies in creating better possibilities for their lives and futures. Environmental organizations and concerned citizens should propose real solutions and back up these solutions with real support. What else can ANCSA corporations do to lift Alaska Native peoples out of poverty while simultaneously protecting the lands and waters that are our lifeblood? We welcome your ideas.

> "Tragically, the mandates of tribes and corporations are conflicted, guaranteeing that we politically fight our own people within a western paradigm in which only one side prevails. Using traditional ways and wisdom, we can show the world that there is a better way."
>
> Ilarion (Larry) Merculieff

ANCSA corporate leaders, likewise, must think outside the box to find ways to make profits while protecting the pristine nature of the lands they hold for their people. Because of the enormous responsibility ANCSA corporations carry to protect the subsistence ways of life of a majority of their shareholders, corporate policy should mandate that when corporate leaders consider major developments that may significantly alter the pristine nature of their land holdings, such proposals must be approved by a majority of shareholders (and their children and grandchildren of voting age) before acting. If the laws of our nation don't allow this action, we should change the laws.

Currently, if Alaska Native shareholders object to a particular economic development project on their lands, their only recourse involves voting out directors who took the action. This response, however, will always be after the fact, after the corporation is contractually bound to the project. Even that response is limited, given that all boards, by law, have staggered terms. It would take two years for unhappy shareholders to vote out the majority of the directors with whom they disagree. Even then, average shareholders who seek change must be able, at great personal expense, to contact all shareholders and communicate in such a way that the message is not invalidated because it is deemed "misleading" according to corporate law. To do this requires a reasonable knowledge of corporate law and the ability to contact over two thousand shareholders (in the case of the smallest regional corporation) or over twenty thousand shareholders (in the case of the largest). At best, replacing board members could prevent similar actions in the future, but such action would not stop what is being done in the present. As a result, it is incumbent upon executives of ANCSA corporations to apply much higher standards to their decisions about Alaska Native lands than what is provided for in U.S. corporate law.

Additionally, there are organized tribal (traditional) governments and regional non-profit corporations in every area of Alaska with a mandate to protect the cultures and ways of life of their constituents. Given the constant threats to the viability of cultures throughout Alaska, for-profit corporations and tribes should ally with each other to protect the life-sustaining ways that allowed Alaska Native peoples to survive and thrive for thousands of years. The alternative is unthinkable. Loss of cultures and languages and the diminishing populations of fish and wildlife will result in profound damage to the health and well-being of families and communities. Tragically, the mandates of tribes and corporations are conflicted, guaranteeing that we politically fight our own people within a western paradigm in which only one side prevails. Using traditional ways and wisdom, we can show the world that there is a better way.

ANCSA corporations, and indeed all corporations, should reject the destructive ways of western corporations and create strategic plans and policies mandating that any development in which they engage must do no lasting harm to the earth or the ways of life of the majority of their shareholders. That is what our Alaska Native ancestors taught us and showed us how to do. We need to do this for all our people, for coming generations, and for the earth on which we depend.

If any corporations can do this, ANCSA corporations can. Our people have survived and thrived for millennia by ensuring that the lands, water, fish, and wildlife upon which all life depends also survived and thrived. This is the legacy of Alaska's Native peoples.

A Third Response: Our Land, Our Decisions, Our Destiny

By Margie Brown

Margie Brown, Yup'ik Eskimo from the Interior village of Takotna, Alaska, is president and chief executive officer of Cook Inlet Regional Incorporated (CIRI), one of twelve Alaska-based regional corporations established by ANCSA to benefit Alaska Natives with ties to the Cook Inlet region. She is an original CIRI shareholder and has served as CIRI's vice president of land and resources, vice president of oil and gas, senior vice president, and Board of Directors member.

The Alaska Native Claims Settlement Act of 1971 (ANCSA or Act) has been a guiding light in my life since its passage. As a young adult I made the decision to become a CIRI shareholder. Not long after, I accepted employment at the company. Over the course of my career, I have worked on and directed many large, even momentous, land ownership and development issues. Today I am honored to serve as president and chief executive officer of CIRI, a corporation that for years has generously provided significant dividends to its shareholders and has played a key role in the history of the young state of Alaska.

It is no exaggeration to use the word "momentous" to describe the Alaska land debates and transactions that took place in the 1960s and 1970s. We were literally carving up the state's three hundred and seventy-five million acres, making decisions that would affect all Alaskans for decades to come. Had we been more experienced in the ways of national policies at the time, I am sure we never would have undertaken such a daunting task. And had we waited even a decade to take up the venture, I am sure it would have been impossible.

ANCSA started as a land struggle between the competing agendas and viewpoints of members of Congress, misaligned state, federal and private interests, and the rights and needs of Alaska Native people. Alaska Native interests were championed by a brilliant and brash group of young Alaska Native leaders who put the hearts and souls of their people first. The effort started after Alaska Native people began to realize the devastating impact the state's land selection of more than one hundred million acres under the Statehood Act would have on their land rights. Settling the land claims issue grew into a national priority after oil was discovered at Prudhoe Bay and developers needed to build the eight-hundred-mile-long Trans-Alaska Pipeline System through the rugged heart of Alaska. These historic events and others provided the unique convergence of circumstances that enabled ANCSA's passage. As a result, the indigenous people of Alaska retained forty-four million acres of land and were granted a cash payment of one billion.

Before ANCSA

To understand ANCSA and its aspirations, it is important to understand the social and economic situation of Alaska Natives before ANCSA. In 1966, the life expectancy at birth of Alaska Natives was 34.5 years, less than half the national average of 70.5 and shorter than that of the residents of such underdeveloped countries as India and Turkey. Native infant mortality was 52.5 per 1,000—more than twice the national average. Alaska Natives had the highest rate of new active tuberculosis cases in the United States, almost twenty times more than the national average. The median Alaska Native family income was below two thousand dollars less than half that of African Americans and about one-quarter that of whites. In fact, this statistic understates the extent of Alaska Native poverty, as rural Alaska prices were the highest in the country.[2]

As Willie Hensley testified before Congress, "We have about 55,000 Natives in Alaska who live in scattered villages through Alaska's 586,400 square miles. About 70 percent of the Native population lives in about 178 villages. We have a subsistence economy of hunting and fishing supplemented by cash incomes earned on various jobs during the short summer season. Seven out of 10 adult Natives have only an elementary education. We have a rapid rate of increase, 29 per 1,000, which is twice that of the United States. The median Native age is 16.3 and 80 percent are less than 35 years of age. The median family size is 5.3. One-half the Native work force of 16,000 to 17,000 is jobless most of the year. The death rate is twice that of white Alaskans; 9.6 deaths per 1,000. The cost of goods in remote parts of Alaska is 74 percent above Seattle costs. Most Alaskan Native families earn less than $2,000 annually, cash." [3]

In other words, Alaska Natives were generally disenfranchised, disrespected, sidelined and often poverty-stricken before ANCSA passed. During hearings on the Act in 1968, then Alaska Attorney General John Rader testified that witnesses who compared living conditions in many Alaska villages to conditions in Appalachia did not take the analogy far enough: "I noticed that they said in the Appalachia testimony—they said that the lack of adequate sewage treatment facilities turned some of the great assets of Appalachia into liabilities. The streams were polluted and so on and so forth. I was talking to a VISTA worker the other day and he said they did not have toilets, sewers or even outhouses. The only trouble with the Appalachia comparison is that it is so mild."

Capitalism and ANCSA

ANCSA has been called a national experiment on a truly grand scale. It uses capitalism and business models to mold the federal government's relationship with Alaska's indigenous peoples. It emerged because Alaska Native and Congressional leaders were united in their rejection of ideas that required the creation of reservations or sustained government oversight, intervention and resource allocation in satisfying Alaska Native claims.

ANCSA drafters settled on a capitalist solution because they thought it provided the most pragmatic solution for meeting all of ANCSA stakeholders' needs. There was some early discussion about using a cooperative model, but capitalism ultimately made more sense because it was thought to be sustainable. Government grants, allocations, and handouts are not sustainable because they generally fail to incentivize permanent solutions and they depend upon political will, which can change with each election cycle. The capitalist business model, on the other hand, offers opportunities for development and increasing value for all stakeholders in the form of jobs, dividends, and economic growth.

The ANCSA drafters are not alone in their view that capitalism is the best way to ensure social and economic justice. The distinguished and talented economist, Hernando de Soto, president of the Institute for Liberty and Democracy in Peru and author of *The Mystery of Capital*, wrote of capitalism: "I am not a die-hard capitalist. I do not view capitalism as credo." But, he continued, to achieve the goals of respect for the social contract and equal opportunity, "...capitalism is the only game in town. It is the only system we know that provides us with the tools required to create massive surplus value."

Capitalism, embedded in ANCSA through the establishment of for-profit Alaska Native corporations, offers self-determination to Alaska Native people who wanted—and got—a model of sustainability. And those who would suggest that ANCSA was wrong-headed, or somehow not in tune with traditional indigenous values, are making generalized statements without evidence.

> "Capitalism...in ANCSA offers self-determination and a model of sustainability to Alaska Native people."
>
> Margie Brown

ANCSA and Alaska Native values

We are fast approaching the 40th anniversary of the Act's passage. This milestone will generate more discussions on the effects of ANCSA, including the suggestion that the corporate model somehow precludes or prevents corporate emphasis on Alaska Native traditions and spiritual values. How much emphasis Alaska Native corporations place on values beyond the bottom line is certainly a decision at the regional and village level, but I submit that no Alaska Native corporation focuses solely on the amount of profit. In fact, some corporations focus a huge portion of their attention on Alaska Native values.

CIRI, for example, has given millions of dollars to create, initially fund, and support a family of nonprofit service providers that serve the social, educational, healthcare, and cultural needs of CIRI shareholders, descendants and other Alaska Natives. These non-profits provide needed services and education programs that reflect traditional Alaska Native values. They also help strengthen families and communities and provide direct or indirect benefits to virtually every Alaskan. And that is just the tip of the iceberg. NANA Regional Corporation uses seventeen Iñupiaq values identified by elders from the NANA region in its daily corporate business decisions. The values of whaling are part of the corporate conscience of the Arctic Slope Regional Corporation. The indigenous value of sharing is also enshrined in ANCSA's resource-revenue sharing requirement—hundreds of millions of dollars have been shared among the corporations over the history of the Act.

Reversing Alaska's business model

Truly noteworthy about ANCSA, however, is that it has turned the traditional Alaska business model on its head. Ever since Alaska was first colonized by Russians, the model has been for outsiders to exploit Alaska's resources and export their profits out of the state. This has been the case with the fur trade, gold mining, and most recently the oil industry. This model is not sustainable, and when the profits play out, the outsiders generally leave and take their revenue with them. With Alaska Native corporations, however, the model is reversed. Alaska Native corporations are doing business in Alaska, throughout the United States and, in some cases, around the world. They bring the profits from Outside back to their Alaska headquarters, using them to create Alaska jobs and pay dividends to Alaska Native shareholders (most of whom live in Alaska).

> "Alaska Native people are not only wise to develop some of our lands, we are the best suited to make decisions about how and when any development should take place."
>
> Margie Brown

Consequently, ANCSA has had the effect of creating wealth that stays in Alaska, benefiting virtually every Alaskan. It has also enabled a diversification of Alaska's economy that would have otherwise been impossible. Michael J. Burns, executive director of the Alaska Permanent Fund, declared that Alaska Native corporations "absolutely control the economic destiny of this state."

Resource debates and decision-making

There are legitimate perspectives on ANCSA that differ from mine and are often voiced when discussing potential resource development. I am not talking about sometimes impassioned debates over whether a particular plan is reasonable and safe for people and the environment. Those sorts of arguments and discussions are appropriate and necessary to ensure that development is truly undertaken in a responsible manner.

ANCSA ensured that Alaska Natives, collectively through their respective Alaska Native corporations, own valuable and significant properties throughout Alaska. Some of these lands are sacred, and some are important for subsistence plants and animals. Truly, some of our lands will never be used for economic development. But decisions as to which lands will be preserved and which will be considered for development are ours to make, collectively, through the boards of directors of each corporation elected by Alaska Native shareholders.

Alaska Native people are not only wise to develop some of our lands, we are the best suited to make decisions about how and when any development should take place. Alaska Natives have traditionally made major decisions based upon what is best for the entire group, not for particular individuals. Collective decision-making has existed for the thousands of years indigenous people have thrived in Alaska. Our corporations today follow similar multigenerational tenets to make decisions, including decisions about developing land in Alaska and their home regions.

ANCSA as a tool

I have been involved in the Alaska Native Claims Settlement Act for more than thirty-five years. My ideas about the Act and its importance to Alaska have matured along as I have matured, and I believe more than ever that Alaska Native corporations play an indispensable role in building a sustainable state economy. I am comfortable with the idea that other types of organizations outside of ANCSA are important to improving Alaska Native peoples' lives. But I fundamentally disagree with any notion that ANCSA and the corporate model it entails are a mismatch for Alaska's indigenous people.

Earlier in my career at CIRI, while I was in charge of CIRI's land and resources department, I was visited by two representatives from the Navajo Nation. They had come to learn how the corporate model was working for CIRI and to explore how the Navajo Nation could set up its own for-profit corporation for the purpose of more actively participating in the oil and gas development that was occurring on the Navajo Reservation.

I frequently think about this meeting and its purpose. Here were representatives of the great Navajo Nation, a nation with so many attributes that Alaska Native people envy: sovereignty, a tribal constitution, and a tribal judicial system, to name three. Yet the Navajo Nation was seeking to establish a for-profit corporation to enhance its peoples' ability to exercise self-determination: what is now, after many years, operating as the Navajo Nation Oil and Gas Corporation.

Conclusion

At its heart, ANCSA is about creating opportunities, not entitlements. ANCSA is government's best attempt to provide Alaska Native people (both original shareholders and their descendants) with opportunities to thrive and succeed in life by using their hard work, intelligence and good luck. ANCSA created Alaska Native corporations so they could stand on their own and empower their shareholders with participation in the state and national economy by doing business, generating jobs, earning profits and distributing appropriate dividends—all the while taking Alaska Native values into account and balancing the needs of current and future shareholders. It is a complex task. But if we succeed, Alaska Native corporations will have a positive influence on Alaska's economic and social development for generations.

---

1. Burgess, Philip, Traditional Knowledge: A Report Prepared for the Arctic Council Indigenous Peoples' Secretariat. Copenhagen: Indigenous Peoples' Secretariat, Arctic Council, 1999.
2. Groh, Clifford J. "Oil, Money, Land, and Power: The Passage of the Alaska Native Claims Settlement Act of 1971," Juneau, Alaska (1976):16.
3. Hensley, Willie. Testimony, Hearings before the Committee on Interior and Insular Affairs, U.S. Senate, on S. 2906, S. 1964, S. 2690, S. 2020 and S. 3586, July 12, 1968, Washington, D.C., Part 2: 561.

READINGS

Please visit our web site at
http://www.uaa.alaska.edu/books-of-the-year/
year08-09/supplemental_readings.cfm
for a variety of supplemental readings

Online Readings

Subsistence

Alaska Federation of Natives. "Subsistence." 2006 Federal Priorities.

Alaska Natives Commission. "Alaska Native Subsistence." Final Report, Volume III.

Alaska Outdoor Council. "Subsistence." AOC Views.

Angasan, Trefon. "Subsistence is What Connects You to the Land."
Essay by Bristol Bay Native Corporation shareholder and former co-chair of the board of directors
of the Alaska Federation of Natives (AFN).

Attungana, Patrick. "Whale Hunting in Harmony." In *Alaska Native News*, June 1985.
Translated remarks by Iñupiaq whaler Kimmialuk (Patrick Attungana).

Burwell, Mike. "The 1976 Decline of the Western Arctic Caribou Herd: Contested Constructions of
Ecological Knowledge." 2006.
Research paper written for UAA anthropology class which details the sources of tension between
rural Native subsistence hunters and non-local game management decision-making entities
and policies.

Burwell, Mike. "Hunger Knows No Law: Seminal Native Protest and the Barrow Duck-In of 1961."
United States Department of the Interior, Mineral Management Service.
Paper presented to the 2004 Alaska Historical Society detailing the protest by Alaska Native people
against federal control over their hunting rights and, therefore, their lands and lives.

Merculieff, Ilarion (Larry). "Heart of the Halibut."
Essay by deputy director of the Alaska Native Science Commission, former Alaska commissioner
of Commerce and Economic Development, and former chairman of the board of the Aleut
Corporation. Describes his coming of age as an Aleut youth by internalizing the wisdom of his
elders for subsistence fishing for halibut.

Pingayaq, Teresa. "Girls Do Not Get Seals!" *Theata* 1, no. 1 (Spring 1973):38–39.
>   Essay by student from Chevak enrolled in English 106 at the University of Alaska, Fairbanks,
>   1973, describing the unusual occurrence of capturing a seal as a girl, since most girls did not hunt.

Climate Change

Cochran, Patricia. "Alaska Natives Left Out in the Cold." *BBC News*, January 5, 2007.
>   Article by Iñupiaq executive director of the Alaska Native Science Commission and the Inuit
>   Circumpolar Conference, arguing that inaction by government agencies is forcing Native
>   communities to adapt to the rapid effects of climate change on their own.

Mustonen, Tero. *Stories of the Raven: Snowchange 2005 Conference Report*. Anchorage: Northern
Forum, June 2006. http://www.uaa.alaska.edu/cafe/upload/StoriesOfTheRaven_06.pdf
>   Report on conference held in Anchorage, Alaska to gather indigenous observations of effects of
>   climate change in Alaska and identify necessary action steps. Published by the Northern Forum,
>   a nonprofit, international organization of subnational or regional governments from ten
>   northern countries.

University of Colorado at Boulder Law School. "Native Communities and Climate Change:
Protecting Tribal Resources as Part of National Climate Policy." 2007.
>   Report describing the disproportionate effects of climate change on indigenous communities and
>   the special problems faced by tribes as a result of these changes.

Indigenous Knowledge

Online course syllabi from the Center for Cross-Cultural Studies, UAF (www.uaf.edu/cxcs)
- Documenting Indigenous Knowledge
- Indigenous Knowledge Systems
- Traditional Ecological Knowledge

Economic Development

Alaska Natives Commission. Economic Issues and Rural Economic Development, 1998–2004. Final
Report, Volume II.

Berger, Thomas R. *Village Journey: The Report of the Alaska Native Review Commission*. October 1985.

Ongtooguk, Paul. "ANCSA: What Political Process?" Alaska History and Cultural Studies Curriculum
Project, Alaska Humanities Forum.

Hard Copy Readings

Subsistence

Blackman, Margaret. *Sadie Brower Neakok: An Iñupiaq Woman.* Seattle: University of Washington Press, 1989.

> Biography of Iñupiaq magistrate and judge Sadie Neakok, who played a key role in the 1961 Barrow "duck-in," when Alaska Natives resisted federal control over traditional hunting rights. Recommended excerpts:
>
> ■ Biographical details (pp. ix–xi).
>
> ■ "Barrow Duck-in and Subsistence Law" (pp. 180–186).

Breinig, Jeane. "Alaska Haida Narratives: Maintaining Cultural Identity Through Subsistence." *Telling the Stories: Essays on American Indian Literatures and Cultures.* Malcolm A. Nelson and Elizabeth Hoffman Nelson, eds. Peter Lang Publishing, 2001.

> Article analyzes the significance of Haida food gathering traditions to the people themselves.

Case, David S., and David A. Voluck. *Alaska Natives and American Laws.* Fairbanks: University of Alaska Press, 2002.

> Major work on the legal status of Alaska Natives.
> Recommended excerpt:
>
> ■ Chapter 8, "Subsistence in Alaska."

Gallagher, Hugh Gregory. *Etok: A Story of Eskimo Power.* St. Petersburg: Vandamere Press, 2001.

> Biography of Charles Edwardsen, Jr., political leader from the Arctic Slope of Alaska and one of the architects of ANCSA.
> Recommended excerpt:
>
> ■ Chapter 8 (pp. 106–123) covers the mid-1960s in Barrow, with a discussion of Barrow's famous "duck-in," and the birth of North Slope Native Association.

Jones, Anore. *Plants That We Eat: Nauriat Niġinaqtuat.* Fairbanks: University of Alaska Press, 2010.

> Description of traditional plants used for food by Iñupiaq peoples.
> Recommended excerpts:
>
> ■ "Berries" (pp. 80–137). Overview of gathering and using berries.
>
> ■ "Poisonous Plants" (pp. 206–220). Warnings on safety concerns with wild plants.

McClanahan, Alexandra J. "April 20, 1995—9th Circuit rules in Katie John's favor." In *Anchorage Daily News,* April 25, 2004.

> Article about Alaska Native victory in legal case about subsistence rights involving Athabascan elders Katie John and Doris Charles of Mentasta.

McClanahan, Alexandra J. "Subsistence Priority Prevails in Election." In *Anchorage Daily News*, November 2, 1982.

>Article describing how Alaska voters defeated a ballot initiative which would have repealed the state's priority for subsistence taking of fish and game in times of shortage.

Merculieff, Ilarion (Larry). "Alaska Native Fish, Wildlife, and Habitat Summit Final Report." Anchorage: RurAL CAP, 2001.

Staton, Norman A. *National Treasure or A Stolen Heritage: Position Paper on the Administrative History of Glacier Bay National Park & Preserve with a Focus on Subsistence.* Juneau: Sealaska Corporation, 1999.

>Recommended excerpt:

- ■ "Foreword" (pp. 4–7). Robert W. Loescher Kaa Toosh Tú explains that the land now encompassed by Glacier Bay National Park belonged to the Tlingit people who used it for subsistence hunting and fishing and that they have been dispossessed.

Climate Change

Merculieff, Ilarion, (Larry). Alaska Native Fish, Wildlife, and Habitat Summit Final Report. Anchorage: RurAL CAP, 2001.

Group portrait of Athabaskan chiefs adorned with traditional garments and ornaments, July 1915.
First row, left to right: Chief Alexander of Tolovana, Chief Thomas of Nenana, Chief Evan of Koschakat, Chief Alexander
William of Tanana. Second row, left to right: Chief William of Tanana, Paul Williams Tanana, Chief Charlie of Minto.

Tribal Government

Are there tribal governments in Alaska?

Are there reservations in Alaska?

Why are there no casinos in the state?

"When [in] 1971, the Native land claims [act] came into law we had a choice of whether to take the land or take the money. And the people very wisely took the land ... We call ourselves a sovereign people. And that's the way it should be, because ... we have our own laws to follow that [have] been in existence before the white man law came into the village, came into the country. And we still follow that. That's a traditional law."
Larry Williams

Are there tribal governments in Alaska?

Editor's note: Issues of tribal status, sovereignty, and jurisdiction are highly complex and in constant motion; they may be advanced, constrained, clarified, or otherwise changed with each new state and federal court ruling. We asked attorney Heather Kendall-Miller to provide brief responses to two of the three questions in this chapter. Ms. Kendall-Miller, Athabascan, is senior staff attorney in the Native American Rights Fund Anchorage office. She argued the Alaska Native sovereignty rights case before the Supreme Court in 1997.

Yes. Alaska's tribes are recognized as sovereign governments with inherent jurisdiction over members and, in some limited cases, nonmembers as well. Recognition of tribal sovereignty acknowledges a tribe's right and power of self-government—attributes all tribes had prior to contact with European nations. Most of the powers of self-government are not bestowed by federal action; instead, court rulings have established that inherent powers of a limited sovereignty have never been extinguished.

Historically, however, the legal status of Alaska's tribes and tribal governments has often been unclear or in dispute. The Alaska Native Claims Settlement Act of 1971 left two questions regarding tribal status unanswered: (1) Do federally recognized tribes exist here? (2) Do they have jurisdiction over members and nonmembers? That is, do the inherent powers of tribes permit them to adopt rules and regulations that are binding on tribal members and nonmembers alike?

Alaska state courts generally resisted and tried to limit tribal status and power in Alaska, but federal courts tended to reach the opposite conclusion. In fact, a number of federal cases establish that the inclusion of Alaska Native groups on a Bureau of Indian Affairs (BIA) listing of tribes nationwide amounts to recognition of inherent authority, entitling Alaska tribes to claim jurisdiction over their members in some legal matters, such as adoptions.

Federal recognition

In 1993, in the closing days of the first Bush Administration, an Opinion of the Solicitor issued by the Interior Department concluded that while tribes existed in Alaska, their territorial jurisdiction had been limited by the Alaska Native Claims Settlement Act. A few months later, in the early days of the Clinton Administration, the BIA revisited the matter and produced a listing that identified 226 federally recognized tribes in Alaska. The BIA listing specifically noted that Alaska Native tribes enjoy the same tribal status as tribes in the lower forty-eight states.

Congressional review of the listing resulted in the Federally Recognized Indian Tribes List Act of 1994, an action that ratified the 1993 listing and effectively endorsed the inclusion of Alaska Native tribes. Under the Tlingit and Haida Clarification Act, Congress also directed the listing of two Alaska Native groups omitted in 1993.

Inclusion on the BIA listing is important not only to support claims of inherent powers, but also to secure federal services reserved for tribes. The 1994 List Act authorized the Indian Affairs Secretary to acknowledge Native American peoples as "tribes" and to annually publish a listing of all such federally recognized entities. The term "Indian tribe" is defined in the Act to mean "any Indian or Alaska Native tribe, band, nation, pueblo, village, or community that the Secretary of the Interior acknowledges to exist as an Indian tribe." It is this backdrop of federal recognition that informs Alaska state courts as they consider matters of inherent powers, sometimes called Native tribal sovereignty.

In 1999, the Alaska Supreme Court acknowledged federal recognition of Alaska tribes in a subsistence fishing case brought by Katie John, an Athabascan elder from Mentasta in the Copper Valley north of Valdez. Among key findings was an acknowledgment that Alaska Native tribes have jurisdiction concurrent with Alaska's state courts over the internal domestic relations of tribal members, even in the absence of federally designated "Indian country."

Are there reservations in Alaska?

Yes, but only one. Nearly all Alaska Native reservations were abolished in 1971 under Section 9 of the Alaska Native Claims Settlement Act. An exception was made for the reservation of Metlakatla in Southeast Alaska. Metlakatla is the only reservation in Alaska today.

After ANCSA, the question still remained: Do former ANCSA lands belonging to a tribe constitute "Indian Country?" Indian Country is the legal term for an area where tribes have specific jurisdiction in matters like policing or regulating alcohol sales. The designation is important, because an area deemed Indian Country can be considered as a "dependent Indian community," affording certain protections under the federal government.

A 1996 United States Supreme Court decision effectively foreclosed the existence of Indian Country in Alaska in most instances. In the case involving the Interior village of Venetie, the court held that two essential characteristics of a dependent Indian

A Brief History

In 1871, four years after the purchase of Alaska, the federal government developed a policy to stop creating both treaties and reservations and hence "Indian Country." An exception was made in 1891 with a Congressional Act to create the reservation of Metlakatla. In 1936, an amendment to the Indian Reorganization Act allowed for the formation of Alaskan "reserves" (as distinct from "reservations") that did not have the "Indian Country" status. The amendment also allowed the half-dozen groups that had formed such reserves rights to tribal land. In 1971, ANCSA extinguished aboriginal rights, including the right to create reservations. As a result of these laws, only one entity in Alaska (Metlatkatla) has the regulatory jurisdiction over community affairs that comes with the legal status of reservations.

Dr. Phyllis Fast

community are that land be set aside for the use of Indians, and that the land—not merely the tribe—be under the superintendence of the federal government. The court concluded that Venetie's lands were neither "validly set apart for the use of Indians as such" nor under the superintendence of the federal government. The ruling did not affect Metlakatla, a few parcels of trust land in Southeast, and restricted Native land in the form of Alaska Native allotments and townsites.

In sum, Alaska's tribes possess inherent jurisdiction over their members, but regulatory jurisdiction over nonmembers has been limited by the *Venetie* case, which held that very little Indian country has existed in Alaska post-ANCSA.

Why are there no casinos in the state?

If you've heard of Indian-owned casinos in the lower forty-eight states, you may have wondered why Native-run casinos don't exist in Alaska. There are two main reasons.

First, to build and run a casino, a Native tribe must own land the federal government designates as within "Indian Country," a legal term referring to land governed by a sovereign tribe but subject to the superintendence of the federal government. In Alaska, only one tribe currently meets this requirement: Metlakatla in Southeast Alaska. Under the Alaska Native Claims Settlement Act (see ANCSA section), all other Native lands—including Native corporation lands—have the same status as private lands, those "fee simple" tracts owned by any Alaska resident or corporation. Native corporations own their lands outright; unlike reservation lands in the lower forty-eight states, they are not under the superintendence of the federal government. Following the 1996 *Venetie* decision, these Native-owned lands are not considered Indian Country and therefore can't be used for casinos.

The second reason is less complicated: Native-run casinos can only operate in states that allow gambling. Currently, Alaska doesn't permit gambling except for limited gaming by non-profit organizations on behalf of charitable causes. Alaska Native non-profits can, therefore, obtain permits for bingo and pull tabs under certain conditions. But casinos remain prohibited under state law.

The question of whether to revise Alaska's gambling prohibitions surfaces every few years, especially as Indian-run casinos in the lower forty-eight states have become proven money-makers. Some Alaska Native people join other voters in the belief that Indian-run casinos generate income necessary for tribal welfare, like funding scholarships or building homes. Still others say that gambling should remain outlawed because it damages families and fuels other addictions.

READINGS

Please visit our web site at
http://www.uaa.alaska.edu/books-of-the-year/
year08-09/supplemental_readings.cfm
for a variety of supplemental readings

Online Readings

Alaska Federation of Natives. "Achieving Alaska Native Self-Governance: Towards Implementation of the Alaska Natives Commission Report." Economics Resource Group and the Institute of Social and Economic Research, University of Alaska Anchorage. May 1999.
> Report addressing such questions as: Can Native self-governance do a better job of dealing with Native problems than non-Native efforts have done? What should be the extent of such governance? What forms should it take?

Anderson, Loren. "What Defines Tribes in Alaska?" 2008.
> Essay by Alaska Native Heritage Center's Alutiiq cultural ambassador.

Cornell, Stephen, and Joseph P. Kalt. "Alaska Native Self-Government and Service Delivery: What Works?" Harvard Project on American Indian Economic Development, 2003.
> Examines the debate that challenges the rights of Native peoples to determine how they will live their lives, manage their resources, and govern their affairs, and specifically addresses the question of what works with respect to the delivery of needed services to Alaska Native people and communities.

Leggett, Aaron. "Native Tribes in Alaska." 2008.
> Essay by Alaska Native Heritage Center's Dena'ina cultural historian.

Mitchell, Donald Craig. "Alaska v. Native Village of Venetie: Statutory Construction or Judicial Usurpation? Why History Counts." *Alaska Law Review* 14, no. 2 (1997):353–441.
> Review of the legislative history determining the sovereignty status of Alaska Natives and the existence of "Indian Country" in Alaska.

Strommer, Geoffrey D., and Stephen D. Osborne. "'Indian Country' and the Nature and Scope of Tribal Self-Government in Alaska." *Alaska Law Review* 22, no. 1 (2005):1–34.
> In response to the questions raised by the 1998 Supreme Court ruling that effectively denied the existence of Indian Country in Alaska, this article offers "1) an analysis of Alaska tribes' current jurisdiction, including areas of uncertainty due to their unique status as 'sovereigns without territorial reach;' and 2) a range of proposals designed to resolve those uncertainties and anomalies by at least partially restoring the 'Indian country' status of, and thus tribal territorial jurisdiction over, some tribal lands in Alaska."

Alaska Natives were legally prevented from establishing mining claims under the terms of the mining act. As this photograph indicates, there were other barriers preventing or discouraging Alaska Natives from participating in the establishment of the social and economic structures of modern Alaska.

Effects of Colonialism

Why do we hear so much about high rates of alcoholism, suicide, and violence in many Alaska Native communities?

What is the Indian Child Welfare Act?

"The children that were brought to the Eklutna Vocational School were expected to learn the English language. They were not allowed to speak their own language even among themselves."

Alberta Stephan

Why do we hear so much about high rates of alcoholism, suicide, and violence in many Alaska Native communities?

Like virtually all northern societies, Alaska suffers from high rates of alcoholism, violence, and suicide in all sectors of its population, regardless of social class or ethnicity. Society as a whole in the United States has long wrestled with problems of alcoholism. As historian Michael Kimmel observes, "… by today's standards, American men of the early national period were hopeless sots…. Alcohol was a way of life; even the founding fathers drank heavily…. Alcohol was such an accepted part of American life that in 1829 the secretary of war estimated that three quarters of the nation's laborers drank daily at least 4 ounces of distilled spirits."[1]

Many scholars have speculated that economic anxiety and social disconnection fueled this tendency towards alcoholic overuse in non-Native men of the early American nation. Non-Native explorers and traders brought alcohol to indigenous Alaskan communities—one venture of colonialism. Higher rates of alcohol and other forms of substance abuse are tied with higher rates of violence in every sector of society.

Alaska's indigenous peoples have experienced colonialism at the hands of the Spanish, British, Russian (1741–1800s), and United States governments (beginning in the 1800s). The terms "colonialism" and "imperialism" refer to the expansion of a nation's powers of governance over lands, cultures, and peoples outside its own national borders, thereby displacing and/or directly dominating the indigenous peoples. With colonialism, populations from the conquering nation generally settle in the new lands; with imperialism, the domination may be through political, economic, and military control alone. In either case, the lands, economies, natural resources, labor—and often the religious, spiritual, educational, and linguistic systems—of the colonized people suffer major disruptions. Although colonizing forces may bring some positive influences, the overall effect is to displace, if not extinguish, pre-existing cultures and societies. Being forced to give up an entire way of life and adapt to a new one often results in self-destructive or destructive behaviors, as communities and individuals cope with the losses and disempowerment that attend colonization.

Alaska Native citizens now experience higher rates of substance abuse and violence (whether directed at others or at themselves, as in suicide) than do non-Natives. Researchers have attributed the high rates of these problems to several factors, mostly related to the impact of colonialism. A few are discussed below.

First, as Harold Napoleon's book *Yuuyaraq* details, the epidemics of smallpox, tuberculosis, and influenza sparked by contact with non-Natives of European ancestry decimated vast proportions of Alaska's Native peoples across the state from the 1700s until the turn of the twentieth century. According to Jared Diamond, Pulitzer prize-winning author of *Guns, Germs, and Steel,* people of European descent developed immunity to these and other diseases through thousands of years of contact with domesticated animals.[2] However, indigenous peoples did not, as there were so few animals in the Americas that were, or even could be, domesticated. As a result, diseases were able to spread through indigenous populations virtually unchecked. Alaska's Native communities have struggled for generations with the emotional and physical trauma these plagues left in their midst.

Second, due to the rapid influx of non-Natives, many Alaska Native cultures have experienced the loss or serious erosion of entire, integrated ways of life involving languages, economies, kinship structures, educational and spiritual practices, community cohesion, and creative expressions. Such dramatic change has stressed many individuals and communities almost to the breaking point. Only one or two generations ago, many rural Native communities were elder-led, subsistence societies—characterized by oral traditions, close-knit extended families, a communal view of the land, ancestral languages, and almost exclusively face-to-face interactions. Almost overnight, many villages became dominated by TV, radio, telephones, computers, cash jobs, snowmobiles, the English language, private property, and youth culture. Deprived of the critical subsistence-provider role played by their fathers, grandfathers, and great-grandfathers, and often lacking entry into the cash economy, many young Alaska Native males struggle with feelings of despair, grief, and anger. The suicide rate for young Alaska Native males is among the highest of any group in the nation.

Third, although many missionaries and educators worked respectfully with and on behalf of Native communities and cultures, others believed the success of their efforts depended upon the destruction of traditional ways. Thousands of Alaska Native youth were exported from their villages to boarding or mission schools far away from home. Although some benefited from the experience, the practice left emotional scars on many others, as Jim LaBelle's essay addresses (see "Readings," Education section). A western education often meant severance of connection to family and culture, as well as direct attacks upon traditional ways of life. Young people were sometimes physically punished for speaking their own languages or honoring their cultural traditions. The personal and cultural injuries and losses inflicted in such cases are still being healed. In addition, as recent media coverage has highlighted, a minority of religious leaders serving in Native villages perpetrated sexual and other forms of abuse against village children. The effects of this abuse then spread to future generations.

Fourth, some groups of Alaska Native peoples have experienced actual slavery and extreme economic exploitation and cultural violence at the hands of colonial powers. As the pieces by Torrey, Corbett, and Merculieff describe, Russian enslavement of the Aleut peoples as workers in the fur seal harvest was replaced in the late 1800s by continuing exploitation at the hands of the United States government. In addition, the internment of the Aleuts during World War II resulted in death and dislocation for many villagers. (In 1988, at the direction of the United Nations, the U.S. government issued a formal apology to the Aleut and Japanese-American people interned during WWII.) These traumas also contribute to the high rates of alcoholism and suicide amongst Alaska's Native peoples, as individuals and communities try to cope with internalized intergenerational pain. Sousan Abadian, Ph.D., discusses the "collective trauma" of indigenous and other peoples in a 2008 *Harvard Magazine* article:

> The social and economic conditions we are seeing–the violence, suicide, addictions, endemic poverty, alcoholism–are to a large extent the symptoms of trauma.... If you attack symptoms separately without attending to the underlying condition, other symptoms will show up. Right now, in many parts of the world, people are doing bits and pieces of what needs to be done to address poverty and violence. But because they come from particular specialties, few take an integrated approach, and almost no one also recognizes the incidence and the effects of trauma. Monetary assistance, housing, better schools, reforming political and legal institutions, are all essential for improving Native people's lives. But all these efforts will fall short if you aren't also channeling resources into addressing trauma.[3]

Lastly, although the Anti-Discrimination Act was passed in 1945, discrimination against Alaska Native people (as well as other minorities) persists in subtle and not-so-subtle ways in modern society. Native people regularly report mistreatment, ranging from long waits for service in business establishments to negative jokes and slurs to threats or incidents of physical or sexual violence. Such mistreatment contributes to the stresses that can fuel episodes of drinking or violence.

Researchers have speculated for years about the possibility of there being a genetic explanation for the higher rates of alcoholism amongst Native Alaskans and indigenous peoples of the "Lower Forty-Eight" and Hawaii. To date, no conclusive evidence exists to confirm this theory.

Native communities and organizations have taken strong steps in recent decades to interrupt these painful cycles and help people recover from the effects of them. There are many resources for people who choose to break cycles of addiction and violence, as well as for those who need help to prevent suicide.

What is the Indian Child Welfare Act?

The Indian Child Welfare Act (ICWA), a law passed by Congress in 1978, requires that Alaska Native or Native American tribes have jurisdiction in foster care or adoption placements involving children of Alaska Native or Native American ancestry. In such cases, a member of the Native tribe to which the child belongs (or is eligible to belong to) determines where the child is placed. Prior to passage of ICWA, welfare agencies, private adoption agencies, and state courts were taking up to 25–35 percent of children of Native ancestry out of their family homes and placing them in non-Native homes.

B.J. Jones, litigation director for Dakota Plains Legal Services, speaks to the issue:

Non-Indian judges and social workers—failing to appreciate traditional Indian child-rearing practices—perceived day-to-day life in the children's Indian homes as contrary to the children's best interests.... In Minnesota, for example, an average of one of every four Indian children younger than age one was removed from his or her Indian home and adopted by a non-Indian couple. A number of these children were taken from their homes simply because a paternalistic state system failed to recognize traditional Indian culture and expected Indian families to conform to non-Indian ways.[4]

With the passage of ICWA, Congress recognized that this placement of so many Native children in non-Native homes was not only deeply disruptive to the lives of the children taken from their families and cultures, but was also a threat to the very viability of Native cultures. By enacting ICWA, Jones states, "Congress was acknowledging that no nation or culture can flourish if its youngest members are removed. The act was intended by Congress to protect the integrity of Indian tribes and ensure their future."[5]

Non-Native families still can and do adopt Native children or take them into foster care. However, the existence of ICWA now makes it more likely that considerable effort will be made to ensure that fewer children lose contact with their families and cultures, and that those who are placed in non-Native homes have a better chance of maintaining strong connections with their traditions and roots.

1. Kimmel, Michael. *Manhood in America: A Cultural History*. Free Press, 1997. 47–48.
2. Diamond, Jared. *Guns, Germs, and Steel*. W.W. Norton, 1997.
3. Lambert, Craig, "Trails of Tears and Hope: 'Collective trauma' takes a ferocious toll on human societies—yet there are pathways to healing." *Harvard Magazine* (March/April, 2008):42–43.
4–5. Jones, B.J. "The Indian Child Welfare Act: The need for a separate law."
http://www.abanet.org/genpractice/magazine/1995/fall/indianchildwelfareact.html

READINGS

Please visit our web site at
**http://www.uaa.alaska.edu/books-of-the-year/
year08-09/supplemental_readings.cfm**
for a variety of supplemental readings

Online Readings

Bissett, Hallie. "I am Alaska Native."
Recent UAA graduate and current MBA student, Dena'ina Athabascan Hallie Bissett discusses her struggle to understand her indigenous identity. She not only comes to terms with her culture, but also realizes how central it is to her life.

Burch, Ernest S., Jr. "The Iñupiat and the Christianization of Arctic Alaska." In *Etudes/Inuit/Studies* 18, nos. 1–2 (1994):81–108.
"In 1890, when the first missions were established in Alaska north of Bering Strait, not a single Native in the region was a Christian. By 1910 Christianity was nearly universal." This paper by a Smithsonian Institute anthropologist documents the course of these changes and presents an explanation of why they occurred as they did.

Central Council of Tlingit and Haida Indian Tribes of Alaska. "A Recollection of Civil Rights Leader Elizabeth Peratrovich, 1911–1958." http://www.alaskool.org/projects/native_gov/recollections/peratrovich/Elizabeth_1.htm
Detailed history of the struggle for civil rights for Alaska Native peoples led by Tlingit activist Elizabeth Peratrovich.

Covenant Restriction. Anchorage, 1948.
List of restrictions regarding property rights drafted in 1948 for Airport Heights subdivision in Anchorage, Alaska, including an article which excludes all nonwhites from owning property in the area. Similar restrictions existed in many other areas of Alaska as well.

Marston, Muktuk. "Beam in Thine Own Eye." *Men of the Tundra: Alaska Eskimos at War*. New York: October House Inc., 1972.
Firsthand documentation of racial injustice and segregation in Nome, Alaska by major in the United States Army Air Corps and delegate to the Alaska Constitutional Convention.

McKinney, Debra. "Shari Huhndorf: Helping the Nation Find a Conscience." LitSite Alaska. http://www.litsite.org

> This review discusses *Going Native: Indians in the American Cultural Imagination* by Shari Huhndorf. The book tells the story of Minuk, who, along with four other polar Eskimos, were abducted by Robert Peary as "specimens" for scientific study in 1897.

Merculieff, Ilarion (Larry). "The Aleut Mouse that Roared, Parts I and II." 2003.

> Personal recollections of Aleut deputy director of the Alaska Native Science Commission and former city manager of St. Paul Island, Alaska. Describes the enormous tensions and devasting social and economic effects brought on by the United States government's abandonment of St. Paul in 1983. The government pull-out came in response to demands from the animal rights movement and a weakened market for the fur seal pelts that had long been harvested by a captive Aleut work force. These two pieces tell the story of a remarkable forty-eight hours out of that tumultuous year.

Peter, Evon. "The Colonization of Alaska Natives."

> Essay by the executive director of Native Movement and former chief of the Neetsaii Gwich'in people in Vashraii K'oo (Arctic Village).

Ulmer, Fran. "Honoring Elizabeth Peratrovich." Speech to the Alaska Legislature, May 1, 1992.

> Speech by then Representative and current UAA Chancellor Fran Ulmer. Honors Tlingit civil rights activist Elizabeth Peratrovich.

Warranty Deed, 1953. Jim Crow Laws.

> Warranty deed which outlines property ownership and dwelling rights for a tract in the Turnagain Heights Subdivision in Anchorage, Alaska. Article 5 refused to allow ownership or dwelling to nonwhites except in the case of servants employed by the owners.

See also "Readings" in Education section.

Hard Copy Readings

Corbett, Helen, and Suzanne Swibold. "The Aleuts of the Pribilof Islands, Alaska." *Endangered Peoples of the Arctic: Struggles to Survive and Thrive*. Milton M.R. Freeman, ed. London: Greenwood Press, 2000. 1–15.

> Describes the unique case of cultural survival by the Aleut/Unungan people, who only attained their full independence and United States citizenship in 1966.

Fienup-Riordan, Ann. "The Yupiit of Western Alaska." *Endangered Peoples of the Arctic: Struggles to Survive and Thrive*. Milton M.R. Freeman, ed. London: Greenwood Press, 2000.

Gallagher, Hugh Gregory. *Etok: A Story of Eskimo Power.* St. Petersburg: Vandamere Press, 2001.
Biography of Charles Edwardsen, Jr., political leader from the Arctic Slope of Alaska and one of
the architects of ANCSA.
Recommended excerpts:

■ Introduction and the first three chapters.

Hope, Herb. "Kiks.adi: Survival March of 1804." *Will the Time Ever Come? A Tlingit Sourcebook.*
Andrew Hope and Thomas Thorton. Fairbanks: University of Alaska Press, 2000.

Huhndorf, Shari M. *Going Native: Indians in the American Cultural Imagination.* Ithaca: Cornell
University Press, 2001.
Shari Hundorf, Ph.D., Yup'ik, is an Associate Professor of English at the University of Oregon.
This former Anchorage resident analyzes systematic European-American projections of their
cultural values and psychological needs onto Native Americans, including Alaska Native people,
with the attendant damaging effects.
Recommended excerpt:

■ "Nanook and His Contemporaries" (pp. 79–128).

Napoleon, Harold, with Eric Madsen. *Yuuyaraq: The Way of the Human Being.* Anchorage: Alaska
Native Knowledge Network, 1986.
Describes the initial effects and continuing impact of the epidemics that afflicted Alaska Native
people from the 1770s through the 1940s. Napoleon's premise is that this death on a massive scale
wiped out culture-bearers and left lasting psychological and spiritual scars. Routes to healing
are also discussed.

Oleksa, Michael. "Elizabeth Wanamaker Peratrovich / Kaaxgal.aat; Roy Peratrovich, Sr. /Lk'uteen."
Haa Kusteeyí, Our Culture: Tlingit Life Stories. Nora Marks Dauenhauer and Richard Dauenhauer, eds.
Seattle: University of Washington Press, 1994. 79–128, 544.
Story of two Tlingit civil rights activists.

O'Neil, Dan. *The Firecracker Boys: H-bombs, Iñupiat Eskimos, and the Roots of the Environmental
Movement.* New York: Basic Books, 2007.
History of the how the federal government considered exploding a series of nuclear bombs south
of Point Hope, Alaska, until the community stopped the project.

Torrey, Barbara Boyle. *Slaves of the Harvest: The Story of the Pribilof Aleuts.* St. Paul Island:
Tanadgusix Corporation, 1978.
Story of the enslavement and exploitation of the Aleut (Unungan) people of the Pribilof Islands and
Aleutian Chain—first by the Russians and then by the United States government (until 1966) in
search of profits from the seal harvest.

Znamenski, Andrei. *Through Orthodox Eyes: Russian Missionary Narratives of Travels to the Denai'na and Ahtna, 1850s–1930s.* Fairbanks: University of Alaska Press, 2003.
> Collection of translations of Russian missionary records that shed new light on the spread of Orthodox Christianity among the Athabascan-speaking peoples of the Cook Inlet, Iliamna, Lake Clark, Stony River, and Copper River areas.

Other Resources

Benson, Diane. *When My Spirit Raised its Hands.*
> One-woman play written and performed by Tlingit artist, writer, and activist Diane Benson. About Tlingit civil rights leader Elizabeth Peratrovich, whose decisive speech before the Alaska Legislature in 1945 helped pass the Anti-Discrimination Act.

Fenno, Mary, Dean Kholhoff, and Terry Dickey. "Forced to Leave: WWII Detention of Alaskan Japanese Americans and Aleuts." Long-term exhibit at the University of Alaska Museum, Fairbanks.

Lekanoff, Anatoly. "Aleut Internment." Audio tape. http://www.alaskool.org/resources/audiovisual/StoriesOfOurPeople.Intro.htm#AleutInternment
> Recollections of an 11-year-old Aleut boy from the Pribilof Islands on the internment of the Aleut people during WWII.

McBride, Rhonda. "Jim LaBelle, Native Boarding Schools." #135. *Consider This.* VHS recording. Channel 7, KSKA program.
> Interview with UAA Alaska Native Studies adjunct professor on his boarding school experience at the Wrangell Institute. Hosted by McBride. 28 minutes.

McBride, Rhonda. *Wrangell Institute: Legacy of Shame.* Award-winning three-part video series. Channel 2, KTUU. 2003.
> Details incidents of repeated sexual abuse at a remote Alaska boarding school. Includes interviews with former students and follows them back to the Wrangell Institute where they participate in a healing convocation sponsored by the Episcopal Archdiocese in Fairbanks.

Williams, Marla. "Aleut Story." Film. 2005. http://www.aleutstory.tv/flm_main.html
> Made-for-television film, documenting the Aleut struggle for human and civil rights and the internment of Aleut citizens during World War II.

Alaska Native Science and Engineering Program (ANSEP) students celebrate in front of their new building on UAA's Anchorage campus. The ANSEP program successfully integrates Alaska Native values into a higher education context. The University of Alaska has graduated 101 Alaska Native scientists and engineers since 2002.

Education and Healthcare

How are traditional Alaska Native ways of educating young people different from non-Native educational practices?

Is the dropout rate for Alaska Native high school and college students higher than rates for other students?

Why are some scholarships for Alaska Native students only?

Do Alaska Native people get "free" medical care?

"The health, housing, and other benefits that are conferred on the Alaska Natives as partial payment for the past takings of land are of importance not only to the Native community but to the economy of the state itself."

Roy M. Huhndorf

How are traditional Alaska Native ways of educating young people different from non-Native educational practices?

In all cultures, the ultimate purpose of an education is to ensure that each new generation is capable of surviving and contributing to society. The current western educational system prepares students to become productive citizens in a global market economy. Very different economies existed in Alaska Native communities prior to contact with Europeans and still exist today in much of rural Alaska. In these subsistence societies, different skills, attitudes, values, and information are prioritized within the indigenous educational process. People make their living directly from the land and water through hunting, fishing, gathering berries, grasses, roots, seeds, nuts, bird eggs, seaweed, and other materials and foodstuffs. Instead of working in an office for the money to purchase food, shelter, and the other necessities of life, people travel in boats, on foot, or, in recent times, on snow machines and all-terrain vehicles to bring home the fish, wildlife, and plants that sustain them. During the summer, people gather food and prepare and store it for winter. In such economies, a highly "place-based" educational system has evolved.

People in subsistence economies need to be able to observe the local natural environment with extraordinary and disciplined attention, noticing both overt and subtle changes in the winds, waters, clouds, temperature, wildlife behaviors, precipitation, and plant life. They must be able to experiment with and innovate in real-life situations, and adapt quickly to changes in environmental conditions. An individual's ability to accurately "read" and respond to the land and water and all its elements—and to place current observations within the context of previous seasons and cycles—may determine whether his or her family will eat that night or that season. The ability to quickly adapt to changing conditions on the tundra or the ocean may determine life or death. Humility and the recognition of and respect for the interdependence of all life forms and systems has been key to survival in Alaska—one of the harshest environments on the planet—and is at the heart of Alaska Native worldviews and traditional Native education.

Until relatively recently, Alaska Native cultures have been exclusively oral, rather than written-based, cultures. Instead of relying on the written word to transfer information and worldviews to the next generation, indigenous Alaskans relied on the stories of hunters, gatherers, and elders for thousands of years. Storytelling played, and still plays, a vital role in passing along cumulative knowledge and wisdom about physical survival, spirituality, and individual and social well-being. Stories are told for many reasons. They provide important information about wildlife and weather; communicate the proper attitudes and actions required for a successful hunt; warn people against foolish behavior that could jeopardize their own survival or the survival of the group; caution against actions that create disharmony in the community; entertain people during long winter nights or at hunting and fishing camps; and convey cultural values. Information is communicated not only through words, but through nonverbal gestures, intonation, and expressions as well. Children in Alaska Native cultures are taught to respect and honor their elders not only as human beings, but also as repositories of generations of knowledge and wisdom critical to the survival of a whole way of life. "When an elder dies," they say, "a library burns."

Accordingly, Alaska Native systems of educating young people differ markedly from dominant non-Native systems of education. Education is "place-based," specific to the locale in which people live; much of it occurs outdoors. It takes place in real-life situations by means of experiential learning. Young people learn how to survive and live properly by observing and learning from the actions and behavior of their elders, and by something akin to apprenticeship under the tutelage of more experienced relatives or community members. They are encouraged to hone and utilize all their observational, intuitive, and sensory skills to succeed at hunting, fishing, and gathering, to survive on land and water, and to create harmony in interpersonal relationships. All lessons—whether about mathematics or linguistics, physics or philosophy—occur within the matrix of community relationships and the natural world, and involve concordant responsibilities within those relationships. Little is abstract: learning is contextualized and rooted within the lives of the students and community. Adults are responsible for providing opportunities for young people to learn, and for providing guidance rather than rote instruction.

This system allows young people to learn as much as they can, in the manner they learn best, and to exercise their own judgment in the context of life and living. Many Alaska Native elders call this the "way of the real human being," providing the next generation with opportunities to learn how to live rather than teaching them how to make a living.

In Native ways of educating, the process of learning—the relationships and attitudes amongst and between the people involved—is considered as important as the content. Many Native educational processes do not involve direct verbal instruction or the correction of mistakes: instead, young people are expected to speak little, listen well, and watch closely, imitating those with more experience and heeding the guidance conveyed in the stories, teasing, and talk of their elders.

Research indicates that instructors in western universities and primary and secondary schools who tie course material to real-life situations, use examples from Alaska Native cultures, encourage small group activities, develop personal relationships with their students, and allow students a range of ways to demonstrate mastery of material, tend to be most effective with Alaska Native students. Research also indicates that what works well for Alaska Native students works well for most students from all backgrounds.

Is the dropout rate for Alaska Native high school and college students higher than rates for other students?

Yes, the retention and graduation rates for Alaska Native and American Indian students at universities in the United States are lower than any other student groups. Currently, for every thirty-five thousand Alaska Native and American Indian students who complete the ninth grade, only one will earn a Ph.D. [1]

Today many Alaska Native college students try to succeed within, or at least to hold onto, both ways of learning. They wish to succeed within the dominant culture and economy while also maintaining strong and deep connections with their cultures, families, and communities. This requires them to "walk in two worlds"—often a difficult task. The same attitudes and behaviors that bring social and educational success in the Native world (e.g., watching closely and saying little) can make things difficult in the western system (where, for example, students are often rewarded for speaking up and penalized for staying silent).

"Dena'ina galeq qbegh qighestle k'usht'a k'el qihtilnesh, qudiq' q'u k'ech' qulyu...The Dena'ina didn't have any books, and they didn't read, but they had beliefs of their own."

Peter Kalifornsky

Some Native elders fear that students who participate in the dominant higher education system risk an atrophying of the skills and worldviews necessary in traditional Native cultures, as well as a loss of connection to village life. To attend a university, many Native students have to relocate to a densely populated urban setting with unfamiliar ways of relating. They also have to eat different foods and, at least temporarily, give up most subsistence activities. Combined with homesickness, personal or family losses back in the villages, language struggles, and financial obstacles, these challenges can make succeeding within a university setting difficult. Urban dwellers may not understand the contrast experienced by Native students moving from small, tight-knit village communities in which people have known each other for a lifetime to the relatively isolated experience of city life. Though this challenge is shared by non-Native students from rural Alaskan communities, the additional cultural differences experienced by many Alaska Native students can make things even tougher.

The troubled historical relationship between Alaska Native cultures and western systems of education also contributes to the challenges faced by many Alaska Native students. For generations, the United States government's policy of forcibly trying to assimilate Native peoples into western society translated into school policies and practices actively hostile towards Native worldviews and students. Students were required to attend mission or board-ing schools far from home where they were often punished harshly for speaking Native languages or participating in traditional activities or customs. Whole generations of people suffered (and continue to suffer) the effects, which range from feelings of disconnection and isolation to a loss of identity to alcoholism or even suicide. A deep mistrust of the educa-tional institutions of the dominant culture is one of the legacies of those traumatic policies and practices.

Why are some scholarships for Alaska Native students only?

Many Alaska Native students who attend colleges, universities, and vocational institutions receive some form of scholarships. Some of the scholarships are from Alaska Native cor-porations, foundations, or tribal organizations. Most Native organizations are interested in encouraging education among their members and their descendants. Generally speaking, they do not offer scholarships to people who are not associated with the corporation or the tribe in some manner.

Alaska Native corporations are private business entities that were created under the auspices of the Alaska Native Claims Settlement Act of 1971. Section 2(b) of the act states that the settlement is to be accomplished "in conformity with the real economic and social needs of Natives." It is this language that is often cited as the reason why Alaska Native corporations concern themselves not simply with bottom line profits, but with the social and economic needs of their shareholders. And it is for this reason that many of the corporations provide scholarships to their shareholders and descendants or provide funding to associated nonprofit entities which, in turn, award scholarships.

Tribal entities often provide scholarship funding from federal grants specifically targeted to Alaska Native students. Because of the taking of land from indigenous peoples by the United States government in years past, a number of benefits have been negotiated through treaties or other agreements. These benefits have included health services, scholar-ship funding, and other social services.

It should be noted that virtually no Alaska Native students garner enough scholar-ship money to pay all their tuition, books, fees, and room and board. Most students consider themselves fortunate to receive $500 to $1,000 a semester in scholarships and still need to avail themselves of student loans and/or part-time employment in order to make ends meet during their college careers. Also, most scholarships have specific standards and guidelines that must be adhered to, such as maintaining a particular grade point average.

Do Alaska Native people get "free" medical care?

Along with questions about corporate dividends, this is perhaps the most commonly asked question about Alaska Native people by non-Natives who live in the state. A better understanding about the history of Alaska Native peoples and American Indians and their relationship with the federal government can clear up the confusion this question represents.

In essence, health care for indigenous peoples in the United States has been "prepaid" through trades of land and resources owned by indigenous nations for basic services from the United States government. In its simplest sense, Alaska Native and American Indian health care today came from a series of government-to-government agreements ("treaties")—essentially business deals—struck between the various tribes and the United States government over the last two hundred years. Indigenous nations ceded their lands, and the resources on or under those lands, to the United States government in exchange for the protection of certain rights and the provision of certain services. Because they were the only groups whose lands were taken by the United States government, indigenous peoples are the only groups for which the United States must—by legal, contractual obligation—indefinitely provide health care services. Established in 1787, this relationship is based on Article I, Section 8 of the Constitution. The organizational vehicle for fulfilling this obligation is the Indian Health Service (IHS).

In the Indian Self-Determination and Education Assistance Act of 1975, Congress stated that "from the time of European occupation and colonization through the 20th century, policies and practices of the Unites States caused and/or contributed to the severe health conditions of Indians." For over two hundred years, the federal government (Congress, presidents, and courts) has acknowledged its responsibility, as well as its legal obligations, to indigenous peoples by passing enabling legislation and providing funding for health care for indigenous citizens. One of the latest pieces of legislation is the Indian Health Care Improvement Reauthorization Act, which has been stalled in Congress for nearly a decade.

The land acquired by the United States in these deals has yielded—and continues to yield—immeasurable value to the American people. Some is still owned and managed by the United States government (national parks, national forests, national wildlife refuges), and is widely used for Americans' business pursuits, such as logging and mining, as well as for recreation. Many of these lands were given or sold to private United States interests. This allowed individual Americans to profit from resources on those lands, through mining or drilling for precious minerals, coal, and oil; farming (both small farms and agri-businesses); paving for the roads and runways of commerce; and building the thousands of towns and cities—including millions of homes—where Americans live and work.

In return for this land, the IHS serves as the principal federal health care provider and health advocate for Indian people, with a goal of raising their health status to the highest possible level. The IHS currently provides health services to approximately 1.5 million Alaska Native and American Indian people from more than 557 federally recognized tribes in thirty-five states. Under Public Law 93-638, the Indian Self-Determination and Education Assistance Act of 1975 (Titles I and III), tribes may choose to take specific program shares or to become totally self-governing. Title III self-governance tribes have total control over their health-related programs. Alaska tribes have taken over all contractible functions from the IHS, including all aspects of health care delivery to the Alaska Native people.

Two things should be noted about the health care received by Alaska Native citizens today.[2] First, the quality of health care received is often far from the "highest possible

David Freeman

level" goal espoused by the IHS. In spite of the best efforts of many medical providers, access to health care is often sporadic and difficult in the nearly two hundred rural Alaska villages. Dental care is even scarcer: Alaska Native individuals suffer rates of dental decay two-and-a-half times higher than other Alaskans. More than one-third of rural Alaska schoolchildren have missed school due to dental pain.[3] For much medical care, people must be flown into regional hospitals in Bethel, Kotzebue, Fairbanks, Sitka, or Anchorage; for major medical care, they must come to Anchorage. When they do, long waiting times and lack of certain providers add to existing stresses. Currently, for example, there is only one oncologist (cancer specialist) in Anchorage to address the needs of a rapidly expanding population of Alaska Native cancer patients. This situation exists in spite of the fact that cancer is the leading cause of death for Alaska Native people, whose rates of death by cancer are increasing at a much higher rate than other Alaskans.[4]

Second, according to its own calculations, the U.S. government falls massively short of providing sufficient funding for the provision of even the most basic health services to Alaska Native and American Indian people. The Federal Disparities Index demonstrates that the Indian Health Service is funded at approximately 60 percent of the level needed to provide basic health care. That figure drops to 40 percent if a wider range of services covered by Medicaid or private insurance plans for other citizens are included: dental, optometry, home health, assisted living, mental health, substance abuse treatment, and rehabilitation treatments. More is spent per inmate in the federal prison system than is available for each American Indian and Alaska Native person for health care.[5]

Why don't other groups in the United States have access to affordable health care? This second question is totally separate from the first. Indigenous citizens of the U.S. have access to health care because they "pre-paid" for it—not with dollar bills but with vast amounts of land that originally contained their homes, food, and the sources of their livelihood. The question of whether and how the United States should provide affordable health care to all other groups in the country (who did not trade land for such services) is a hugely important, but unrelated, question. Issues related to insurance, Medicare/Medicaid, health care costs, access, and disparities, can only be grappled with separately by getting involved in local, state, and national political processes.

Response courtesy of the Southcentral Foundation.

1. Postsecondary institutions in the United States: Fall 2003 and degrees and other awards conferred: 2002-03. National Center for Education Statistics, 2005.
2. On a separate topic, it should also be noted that the Alaska Native Medical Center submits claims to private insurance companies for services rendered for those Alaska Native people who have private insurance—in other words, when they can, Alaska Native people pay their own way, on top of their pre-paid health services.
3. Rural Alaska's Dental Access Problem. Alaska Native Tribal Health Consortium. http://www.anthc.org/cs/chs/dhs/upload/Access6-6-06sos5.0.pdf
4. Cancer in Alaska Natives 1965–2003: A 35-Year Report. Office of Alaska Native Health Research, Alaska Native Epidemiology Center, Alaska Native Tribal Health Consortium, January 2006. Pages 1-4 http://www.anthc.org/cs/chs/oanhr/upload/Cancer_Incidence_35-Year_Report.pdf.
   Also, "Comprehensive Cancer Plan for the Alaska Native Tribal Health System. 2005-2010," Alaska Native Tribal Health Consortium Program. www.anthc.org. 45.
5. Personal Health Services Funding Disparities. Indian Health Service, January 2007. info.ihs.gov/Files/FundingDisparity-Jan2007.doc.

READINGS

Please visit our web site at
**http://www.uaa.alaska.edu/books-of-the-year/
year08-09/supplemental_readings.cfm**
for a variety of supplemental readings

Online Readings

Alaska Natives Commission. Final Report, Volume III. Native Tribal Government, Section II, Tribal Sovereignty and Federal Indian Law and Policy.

Barnhardt, Ray, and Angayuqaq Oscar Kawagley. "Indigenous Knowledge Systems and Alaska Native Ways of Knowing." In *Anthropology and Education Quarterly* 36, no. 1 (2005):8–23.
    Article by Dr. Oscar Kawagley (born at Mamterilleq, now known as Bethel) and Dr. Ray Barnhardt.

Cotton, Stephen. "Alaska's Molly Hootch Case: High Schools and the Village Voice." In *Educational Research Quarterly* 8, no. 4 (1984):30–43.
    Documents the landmark court case in 1972 that led to the establishment of high schools in 126 villages and effectively spelled the end of the boarding school program.

Dinwoodie, Dawn. "CIRI's Native Pride Program." LitSite Alaska. http://www.litsite.org
    Program to help address Native dropout rate.

Haycox, Stephen. "Desegregation in Alaska's Schools: Alaska Yesterday." In *Anchorage Times*, January 26, 1986.
    Article by UAA professor of history Stephen Haycox outlines the historical problems of segregation in Alaska schools and the struggle toward integration.

Hirshberg, Diane, and Suzanne Sharp. *Thirty Years Later: The Long-Term Effect of Boarding Schools on Alaska Natives and Their Communities.* Institute for Social and Economic Research, University of Alaska Anchorage, 2005.
    Study that examines the positive and negative impacts of sixty-one Alaska Native individuals who attended boarding schools or boarding home programs between the late 1940s and early 1980s.

Hopson, Eben. "Iñupiaq Education." Mayor's address on education, North Slope Borough, Barrow, Alaska, 1975.
    Speech by Iñupiaq leader Eben Hopson, chief architect of the Inuit Circumpolar Conference, about the need for the Iñupiat to maintain control over the education of their children.

Ilutsik, Esther. "Oral Traditional Knowledge: Does it Belong in the Classroom?" In *Sharing Our Pathways* 7, no. 3 (Summer 2002). http://www.ankn.uaf.edu/SOP/SOPv7i3.pdf

Kleinfeld, Judith, and Joseph Bloom. *A Long Way From Home: Effects of Public High Schools on Village Children Away from Home.* Center for Northern Educational Research and Institute of Social, Economic and Government Research, University of Alaska, 1973.
> Study of the discontinued state regional boarding programs for Alaska Native high school students which required most village students to attend school far from home.

LaBelle, Jim. "Boarding School Historical Trauma among Alaska's Native People." National Resource Center for American Indian, Alaska Native, and Native Hawaiian Elders. October 2005. http://elders. uaa.alaska.edu/reports/yr2_2boarding-school.pdf
> UAA adjunct professor examines the traumatic impacts of the Wrangell Institute Boarding School and the Episcopal Church of Alaska's significant role in implementing, and organizing a "Healing Convocation" for some of its parishioners. Discusses broader aspects of historical trauma among Alaska Natives, 1880s–1900s. Topics include the introduction of western illnesses and diseases, boarding schools, and forced Christianity. The author's personal experience informs the essay.

McClanahan, Alexandra J. "A Look Back in History: Clock is Ticking On Saving Jesse Lee Home." http://jesseleehome.net/history

Nelson Act. January 27, 1905.
> This legislation created racially segregated schools in Alaska.

Ongtooguk, Paul. "Aspects of Traditional Iñupiat Education."
> Discussion of some of the myths and realities of traditional Iñupiaq education by UAA Assistant Professor of education Paul Ongtooguk, an Iñupiaq from Northwestern Alaska.

Other Web Sites of Interest

Alaska Native Knowledge Network Curriculum Resources. http://www.ankn.uaf.edu
> Resources for compiling and exchanging information related to Alaska Native knowledge systems and ways of knowing.

Hard Copy Readings

Education

Barker, Robin. "Seeing Wisely, Crying Wolf: A Cautionary Tale on the Euro-Yup'ik Border." *When Our Words Return: Writing, Hearing and Remembering Oral Traditions of Alaska and the Yukon.* Phyllis Morrow and William Schneider, eds. Logan: Utah State University Press, 1995. 79–97.

Blackjack, Ada, and Billy Blackjack Johnson. Papers in UAA Archives: Billy Blackjack Johnson (b. 1924) 1923, 1929, 1946, 1969–1986, 1990–1997.

> Collection relating to various Alaskan Native organizations in which Billy B. Johnson was involved, as well as papers relating to his personal life, his mother Ada Blackjack Johnson, and the Jesse Lee Home, a Methodist orphanage and school. The Jesse Lee Home, about which Johnson wrote a book, became home to many Alaska Native children "often sent there as a result of the ravages of epidemics of influenza and tuberculosis that hit villages for years throughout Alaska."

Case, David S., and David A. Voluck. *Alaska Natives and American Laws*. Fairbanks: University of Alaska Press, 2002.

> Major work on the legal status of Alaska Natives peoples.
> Recommended excerpts:
> ■ "Dual Systems of Education."
> ■ "The White v. Califano Approach."

Dauenhauer, Richard. *Conflicting Visions in Alaskan Education Revisited*. Anchorage: Tlingit Readers, Inc., Alaska Native Knowledge Network, 1997.

> Documents the life and work of two men, John Veniaminov and Sheldon Jackson, who had profound and differing influences on the history of education in Alaska and its impact on Alaska Native peoples and cultures.

Gooden, James R. "The New Teacher." In "Miss Thompson's Bigotry Really Hurt." In *Tundra Times*, July 26, 1989.

> Piece written by James Gooden, Iñupiaq from Kiana, Alaska, for a distance-delivered UAA writing class, which describes the author's experiences at a Fairbanks elementary school in the late 1950s.

Okakok, Leona. "Education: A Lifelong Process." *Native Heritage: Personal Accounts by American Indians, 1790 to the Present*. Arlene Hirschfelder, ed. MacMillan, 1995.

> Leona Okakok, Iñupiaq and former deputy director of the North Slope Borough School District woman, discusses Iñupiat educational philosophy in this excerpt from an article published in the Harvard Education Review in November 1989.

Health

Barry, Doug, and Libby Roderick. "Della Keats: Hands of a Healer." *Alaska Woman Magazine*, 1982.

> Profile of renowned Iñupiaq healer who blended traditional Native and modern western healing practices.

Fortuine, Robert. *Chills and Fevers: Health and Disease in the Early History of Alaska*. Fairbanks: University of Alaska Press, 1992.

> History of Western diseases and medicine among Alaska Native peoples.

Four generations of Cup'ik doll makers: Rosalie Paniyak (lower left),
Ursula Paniyak-Irvin (upper left), Janice Tamang (upper right), and
Jaderiane Paniyak (lower right) at the AFN Craft Fair, Anchorage.

The Future

What does the future look like for Alaska Native communities and cultures?

Where do we go from here?

"Native people in every region of the state fundamentally desire more control over their lives. To the greatest extent possible, Native communities should have the power to address conflicts, educate children, and make decisions about their own lives themselves."

Ilarion (Larry) Merculieff

What does the future look like for Alaska Native communities and cultures?

Over the past several hundred years, and particularly in the last century, Alaska's Native communities and peoples have faced, adapted to, and survived an onslaught of change and challenge. Epidemics of flu and tuberculosis decimated Alaska's indigenous populations in the early 1800s and 1900s, wiping out as much as 60 percent of the population. Throughout the 20th century, the burgeoning non-Native population diminished Native visibility—Alaska Native people now represent 16 percent of the total state population, whereas in 1930 they constituted over half the state's population. The accelerated search for oil, minerals, timber, and fish; the increased presence of sports hunting and fishing interests; the impact of western religions and boarding schools; the selection of lands by the state; the encroachment of television, the Internet, and other distance technologies into village life; majority rule laws and representation—all these factors and more have required Native peoples to adapt rapidly as traditional ways have been eroded and modern, non-Native forces have gained strength.

Challenges abound for the future. What does it mean to be Alaska Native in a world in which fewer and fewer elders remember the old ways, speak their ancestral languages, and live fully subsistence-based lives, while more and more young people intermarry, move out of the villages, and adopt "western" values and lifestyles? Where are Native corporations headed? How will climate change continue to impact Native villages and the wildlife on which they depend? Can Alaska's legal, political, scientific, and educational leaders learn from the wisdom of Native elders in terms of shaping the future? All this remains to be seen.

Some things are relatively certain. Climate change will profoundly and adversely affect all subsistence-based communities as sea ice, snow, and fresh and salt water levels change, riverbank erosion increases, fish and wildlife populations plummet or dramatically change their migratory patterns, storms intensify, and new species are introduced. Some areas will be more affected than others. Some villages will be forced to move to other locations if they can muster the financial and technical wherewithal to do so. Barge and air transportation costs are escalating, and essentials such as home heating fuel and groceries are becoming more costly. In response to skyrocketing petroleum-based fuels, and lacking alternatives, some smaller Native villages will either have to return to more basic means of survival, or simply disappear as their populations migrate to less expensive regional hubs or urban centers. It is likely several villages will band together to create new and larger communities. "Urban Natives" may not keep close ties to the lands, waters, and fish and wildlife; thus, cultural erosion may intensify.

As Alaska's non-Native population increases and more people migrate to the state, Alaska Native voting power will continue to diminish, with several potential implications.

Philip Blanchette and John Chase sing and beat traditional Yup'ik drums
at a dedication ceremony at the Alaska Native Heritage Center.

Alaska Native communities may not be able to prevent legislative and state administrative initiatives that are adverse to Alaska Native and rural Alaska interests. For example, the legislature may change laws to, in effect, force unincorporated boroughs to incorporate. Such an action would, in turn, result in taxation of lands, including lands originally selected for subsistence and other cultural (non-commercial) purposes. The state could create legislation that further emasculates tribal powers or promulgate laws and regulations increasingly hostile to Alaska Native subsistence rights, or use state funds to lobby the federal government to change subsistence protection laws or legally challenge such laws in courts. Politicians may no longer court the Alaska Native constituency if it is no longer a potential "swing vote" in statewide elections, further diminishing Alaska Native influence in the political arena.

Yet, for millennia, Native communities and cultures have remained resilient and fought to protect the integrity of and a deep connection to the traditional ways of their ancestors. With the passage of the Alaska Native Land Claims Act in 1971, Alaska Native communities retained some of their lands and became major political and economic forces within the state and beyond. New movements for tribal sovereignty and community wellness have spread statewide, blossoming in some regions more than others. Efforts to document and revitalize Native languages have sprung up throughout Alaska, as well as initiatives to ensure that Native elders pass their knowledge and wisdom to new generations. Native artists blend traditional art forms with modern innovations to create exciting new works. Subsistence hunters, fishers, and gatherers are adapting new technologies to ancient practices. Young Native leaders are finding ways to take advantage of new opportunities while embodying elders' values.

Whatever the case, the future will depend on the will, strength, and intentions of new generations of Alaska's Native peoples, and the degree of support they can muster from allies in the non-Native community. As always, in Alaska, it is clear that we shape our collective future by the decisions we make and the actions we take today.

Where do we go from here?

Editor's note: Although many Alaska Native people share common experiences and values, no one voice can speak for them all, as Alaska Native leaders have consistently expressed and as the varied viewpoints articulated in this book make abundantly clear. However, in an effort to leave readers with a clear picture of the kinds of steps that could be taken to ensure a more equitable future, we asked one of our contributors, Larry Merculieff, to summarize a few highlights of what many in the Native communities have been working to achieve over several decades.

Where Do We Go From Here? One Vision for the Future
By Ilarion (Larry) Merculieff

Although Alaska Native peoples and leaders have multiple visions for the future, I believe most of us agree that the following actions would greatly improve relations between Natives and non-Native people and move us towards a more culturally, socially, and economically equitable and vibrant Alaska.

■ Greater Local Control

Native people in every region of the state fundamentally desire more control over their lives. Village life is vastly different from city life, and Native values are often at odds with non-Native values. Laws need to be modified so that non-Native city-based laws aren't applied inflexibly and insensitively to situations encountered in Native village life. To the greatest extent possible, Native communities should have the power to address conflicts, educate children, and make decisions about their own lives themselves. Where this is not possible, regulations should be designed to be fully sensitive to the need to protect the cultural integrity and subsistence ways of life of the people they regulate. Lacking such regulations, a village officer often has no choice but to arrest the elder who has taken a three-foot halibut to feed himself, or the elders (like those in Fairbanks arrested some time ago) who take a road-killed moose to use in a potlatch. There is no justice in such actions. There needs to be more room for local decision-making.

■ More Equitable Allocation of Resources

Both Native and non-Native rural citizens agree that rural Alaskans often get the short end of the stick when it comes to the allocation of state resources. For example, Alaskan cities tend to have highly trained and highly paid law enforcement officers, ensuring a high level of security for most citizens. In rural Alaska, communities are forced to rely on the services of Village Police and Safety Officers (VPSOs), who are often poorly paid and inadequately trained. In addition, there are often few Native people in these jobs, so non-Natives disproportionately exercise authority over Native citizens, a situation that contributes to tensions in the village. Allocating resources more equitably would result in higher levels of security and harmony in many rural Native communities.

■ Educational Programs about Native Ways of Life

Efforts to educate the public on the importance and significance of Alaska Native cultures would help make the public into more of an ally than an adversary when it comes to protecting subsistence ways of life and the integrity of Native cultures. Currently, many people—particularly new immigrants to Alaska—make decisions and form opinions about key issues in a virtual vacuum. A better understanding of who Native peoples are—our histories, our cultures, our values, our ways of life—could do much to create an environment in which we work together to ensure that all Alaskans, Native and non-Native, can peacefully coexist.

■ True Partnerships in Decision-Making Bodies That Affect Our Lives

Native citizens deserve to be included as full partners at all levels of government decision-making and on all regulatory and other bodies that make decisions affecting Native communities and ways of life. Currently, Native people are most often consigned to "token" seats on advisory boards and commissions that have enormous impacts on our daily lives and our futures. This needs to change.

■ Greater Equity in Legal and Educational Systems

There is currently little in the Western legal system that recognizes and gives legal standing to communal approaches and structures—the basis for the traditional Native way of life. Instead, the legal system has an almost exclusively individualistic orientation. The result can be needless conflict. For example, Native hunters who obtain fish or game for an entire community have been cited for exceeding individual game limits. Recognition of communal structures within the legal system would permit Native people to live in a way that best supports their communities and honors their cultural values.

Similarly, our educational systems need to have more respect and support for Native ways of teaching, learning, and living. Native communities desire allies who will support local initiatives to restore or enhance cultural programs in village schools—not as "poor stepchildren" to the "mainstream" educational programs, but as fully equal, fully supported aspects of our school systems.

■ Environmental Justice

Like ethnic minorities elsewhere in the U.S., Alaska Native peoples tend to suffer a disproportionate impact from environmentally dangerous actions taken by governments at all levels. As just one example, many old contaminated military sites are located adjacent to Native villages and subsistence lands. More resources need to be devoted to help communities clean up these toxic sites and to recover from the negative impacts they have had on the local people, habitat, and wildlife. Great care needs to be taken to ensure that Native peoples and communities are fully involved and have sufficient resources to protect themselves as fully as possible from future effects of climate change, environmental toxins, and other health and environmental threats.

■ Support for Economic Survival and Development

Native communities—and the entire state—would be well-served if the general leadership and the public demonstrated a higher level of sensitivity to the harsh economic realities of much of rural Alaska life and offered more assistance in dealing with the daunting issues facing rural communities struggling to survive economically. The entire state benefits when Native communities survive and thrive.

Janie and Jonna Michel, of Kwethluk.

ADDITIONAL RESOURCES

Alaska Federation of Natives
www.nativefederation.org/
Statewide Native organization which seeks to promote the cultural, economic and political voice of the entire Alaska Native community.

Alaska Native Brotherhood/Alaska Native Sisterhood
http://www.grandcampanb.org/
Oldest Indian organization in the United States, formed in 1912 to promote and protect the interests of Alaska Native peoples.

Alaska Native Heritage Center
www.alaskanative.net/
Educational and cultural institution that provides workshops, demonstrations, indoor exhibits, and outdoor village sites.

Alaska Native Knowledge Network
http://www.ankn.uaf.edu/
Resources for compiling and exchanging information related to Alaska Native knowledge systems and ways of knowing.

Alaska Native Language Center
http://www.uaf.edu/anlc/
Center for the research and documentation of Alaska Native languages.

Alaska Native Science Commission
www.nativescience.org/
Clearinghouse, information base, and archive for research related to the Alaska Native community.

Alaska Native Youth Media Institute
http://www.knba.org/training/tc_anymi.php
Program offered through radio station KNBA in Anchorage to help Alaska Native students explore careers in the media.

Alaskool
www.alaskool.org/
Online materials about Alaska Native history, education, languages and cultures.

Alaska Native History Timelines

The following timelines include key events that occurred after contact with Western influences. We hope your research will help make them even more accurate and complete and, more importantly, inform us all about the rich histories of Alaska's Native peoples in the thousands of years before contact.

Alaskool:
http://www.alaskool.org/cgi-bin/java/interactive/timelineframe.html

Statewide Library Electronic Doorway (SLED) Alaska's Digital Archives:
http://vilda.alaska.edu/cdm4/timeline.pdf

Cultural Sensitivity

Alaska Native Knowledge Network Curriculum Resources
http://www.ankn.uaf.edu/curriculum/resources.html

Alaska Standards for Culturally Responsive Schools
http://www.ankn.uaf.edu/publications/standards.html

McIntosh, Peggy. "White Privilege and Male Privilege: A Personal Account of Coming to See Correspondences through Work in Women's Studies." Wellesley College Center for Research on Women, Massachusetts, 1988.
Seminal article on becoming aware of and responding to institutional racism.

Pollock, Mica, ed. *Everyday Antiracism: Getting Real About Race in School.* The New Press, 2008. Recommended excerpt: Chapter by UAA education professors Paul Ongtooguk and Claudia Dybdahl offers concrete, realistic strategies to teach more accurately about indigenous cultures in schools.
http://www.thenewpress.com/index.php?option=com_title&task=view_title&metaproductid=1366

Roderick, Libby. *Steps Towards Creating Inclusive Adult Learning Environments: A Manual for Instructors and Facilitators.* 1999.
Research-based ideas for creating more inclusive learning environments for students of all ethnic backgrounds.

SOURCES: QUOTATIONS

Identity, Language, and Culture

Boraas, Alan. In *Anchorage Daily News,* July 7, 2002.

Buretta, Sheri. "Malrugni Yuuluni: Walking in Two Worlds With One Spirit." Alaska Native Corporations Annual Economic Report. Association of ANCSA Regional Corporations Presidents/CEOs, 2005.

Fast, Phyllis. "Alaska Native Language, Culture and Identity." 2008. http://www.uaa.alaska.edu/books-of-the-year/year08-09/supplemental_readings.cfm

Swan, Clare. Cook Inlet Tribal Council Board Chair. *Dena'ina: Nat'uh Our Special Place.* Alexandra McClanahan, Aaron Leggett, and Lydia L. Hays, eds. Anchorage: Cook Inlet Tribal Council, 2007.

Alaska Native Claims Settlement Act and Corporations

Shively, John. "Alaska Native Corporations and Native Lands." Rocky Mountain Mineral Law Foundation. 4–5.

Wright, Don. Testimony, Hearings before the Senate Committee on Interior and Insular Affairs, April 29, 1971. 475.

Subsistence and Relationship to Land, Waters, and Wildlife

Angapak, Nelson. Quoted in *Stories of the Raven: Snowchange 2005 Conference Report.* Tero Mustonen, ed. Anchorage: Northern Forum, June 2006. 10. http://www.uaa.alaska.edu/cafe/upload/StoriesOfTheRaven_06.pdf

Brown, Margaret L. *Dena'ina: Nat'uh Our Special Place.* Alexandra McClanahan, Aaron Leggett, and Lydia L. Hays, eds. Anchorage: Cook Inlet Tribal Council, 2007.

Dinwoodie, Dawn. *Growing Up Native in Alaska.* Alexandra J. McClanahan, ed. Anchorage: CIRI Foundation, 2000. 253–271.

Hopson, Eben. Quoted in "Hunger Knows No Law." Michael Burwell. http://www.uaa.alaska.edu/cafe/upload/Hunger-Knows-No-Law-AAAMarch2005Last.pdf

Huntington, Orville. Quoted in *Stories of the Raven: Snowchange 2005 Conference Report,* Tero Mustonen, ed. Anchorage: Northern Forum, June 2006. 14–15. http://www.uaa.alaska.edu/cafe/upload/StoriesOfTheRaven_06.pdf

Rock, Rex. *Growing Up Native in Alaska.* Alexandra J. McClanahan, ed. Anchorage: CIRI Foundation, 2000. 91–100.

Shively, John. Final Report, Volume III. Alaska Native Commission. October 28, 1991. 11.

Stephan, Alberta. *The First Athabascans of Alaska: Strawberries.* Pittsburgh: Dorrance, 1996.

Tribal Government

Williams, Larry. *Village Journey: The Report of the Alaska Native Review Commission.* Thomas R. Berger. New York: Hill & Wang, 1985.

Effects of Colonialism

Stephan, Alberta. *The First Athabascans of Alaska: Strawberries.* Pittsburgh: Dorrance, 1996.

Education and Healthcare

Huhndorf, Roy M. *Reflections on the Alaska Native Experience.* Anchorage: CIRI Foundation, 1991. 36.

Kalifornsky, Peter. *A Dena'ina Legacy: K'TI'egh'I Sukdu: The Collected Writings of Peter Kalifornsky.* Fairbanks: Alaska Native Language Center, 1991. 73.

The Future

Merculieff, Ilarion (Larry). "Where Do We Go From Here? One Vision for the Future." 2008.

INDEX

land. *See also* Alaska Native
  Land Claims Act
  as an asset, 45
  development of, 46
  importance of, 33
  indigenous occupation of, 21
  making a living with, 78
  protection of, 19, 43, 61
  respect for, 44
  taxation on, 45, 91
  value of, 82
languages
  of Alaska Natives, 4, 6–8,
    24, 44
  English, 67
  loss of, 50
  preserving, 24, 92
  punishment and, 69
laws. *See also* specific laws
  casinos and, 64
  corporate, 45–46
  "English-only," 7
  land and, 49
  majority rule, 90
  modifications of, 93
  subsistence protection, 91
  values and, 44–45
legal system, 94
life expectancy, 52
local control, 93
local natural environments, 78
logging, 38–55
males, 69
map of Alaska, *3*
McPhee, John, 43
Medicaid, 84
medical care, 82–84
medical care for Alaska
  Natives, 82–84
Medicare, 84
Merculieff, Ilarion (Larry),
  44–50, 49, 89, 92–94
Metlakatla, 63–64
Michel, Janie, *95*
Michel, Jonna, *95*
migration, 20
Miller, George, 21

mining, 38–55, *66*
mission schools, 69
Mystery of Capital, The (de
  Soto), 53
NANA Regional Corporation, 53
Napoleon, Harold, 68–69
natural gas, 38
Navajo Nation Oil and Gas
  Corporation, 55
NIMBYs (Not In My
  Backyarders), 40
Nixon, Richard, 21
non-Natives
  adoption of Alaska Natives
    and, 71
  alcohol and, 68
  conservation organizations of,
    42–43
  corporations of, 22, 44
  diseases from, 68–69
  education and, 78–79
  influx of, 5, 69
  laws of, 93
  population of, 3, 90–91
  rights of, 30–32
  vision of Alaska, 39
nonprofit corporations, 39
North Pacific Fishery
  Management Council, 49
Notti, Emil, *21*
offshore drilling, 42
oil
  development of, 5, 42
  discovery of, 51
  drilling for, 38, 42
  revenues from, 22
Ongtooguk, Paul, 38–43
oral history, 7, 69, 78
Paniyak, Jaderiane, *88*
Paniyak, Rosalie, *88*
Paniyak-Irvin, Ursula, *88*
partnerships, 94
Paukan, Moses, *21*
plagues, 68–69
plants, 37
population, 2, 3, 90
poverty, 40, 49, 52

prison system, 84
Prudhoe Bay, 51
pull tabs, 64
quality of life, 40
racism, 35
regional tribal governments, 40
reindeer herding, 33
reservations, 63–64
reserves, 63
resources, equal allocations of, 93
restaurant operations, 47
revenues from oil, 22
road-kill, 93
Rock, Rex, 30
rural communities, 46
rural preference, 32
Russia, 20, 54, 69
salmon, 37
Samuelson, Harvey, *21*
Schmidt, Serenity, *x*
scholarships, 81
sea ice, 35–37
self-determination, 24, 55
self-government, 62
settlement payments, 22
sewage treatment facilities, 52
shareholders
  Alaska Natives as, 22, 24,
    41–42
  concerns of, 25
  financial gains for, 4, 23, 39,
    44, 51
  laws and, 40–41, 49–50, 54
  needs of, 55, 81
  protection of, 45
shellfish, harvesting, 30–32
Shively, John, 25
small boats, 47
social disconnection, 68
societies, subsistence, 78
sovereignty, tribal, 62, 92
Spein, Peter, *28*
Spein, Vera, *31*
sports fishing, 32, 49
sports hunting, 32
Statehood Act, 51
Stephan, Alberta, 29, 67

stewardship, 33
storytelling, 12, 14, 78
subsistence
  camps, 44
  economies, 78
  fishing, 44, 63
  hunting, *28,* 30–32, 44
  societies, 78
  ways of life, 44, 49
substance abuse, 68
suicide, 68–70
survival, 78, 90
sustenance, 33
Swan, Clare, 5
Tamang, Janice, *88*
Tanana, Paul Williams, *60*
tattoos, face, *x*
taxation of land, 45, 91
technologies, new, 30, 40, 48
Thomas of Nenana (Chief), *60*
Thompson, Morris, *21*
Tlingit and Haida Central
  Council, 3
Tlingit and Haida Clarification
  Act, 63

tourism, 47, 48
traders, 20, 68
traditional knowledge and
  wisdom, 35–36, 50
traditional ways of knowing,
  35–36
traditional ways of life, *60,* 69
traditions. *See* elders; languages
Trans-Alaska Pipeline System,
  5, 20, 51
trauma, 70
treaties, 82
tribes
  federally recognized, 62
  governments of, 40, 62–63
  sovereignty of, 62, 92
  welfare of, 64
Trigg, Barbara, *21*
Tundra Times, 3
unincorporated boroughs, 91
University of Alaska, 41, *76*
Urban Natives, 90
values, 2, 4, 93
Venetie, 63–64

Village Police and Safety
  Officers (VPSOs), 93
violence, 68–70
Wallis, Tim, *21*
water, 33, 78
water levels, 37
waves, 37
wealth, 54
weather conditions, 37
well-being, 31, 44, 92
whaling, 30
wild foods, harvesting, 30–32, 35
wilderness, 39
wildlife. *See also* animals
  changes in, 35–36
  diminishing populations of, 50
  respect for, 44
William of Tanana (Chief), *60*
Williams, Larry, 61
wind power, 48
World Eskimo Olympics, *9*
World War II, 70
Wright, Don, 19
youth, 69, 79, 80–81
Yuuyaraq (Napoleon), 68–69